M000283422

ARKANA

# Return from death

**Margot Grey** is a Humanistic Psychologist with an abiding
interest in the spiritual aspects of human nature. She is a Fellow of
the World Association of Social Psychiatry and founder of the
International Association for Near-Death Studies in the United
Kingdom. She recently undertook a research project to examine
cross-cultural similarities between near-death experiences in
England and those reported in the American investigations. She
lives in London where she is in practice as a psychotherapist.

# Return from death

## An Exploration of the
## Near-Death Experience

MARGOT GREY

ARKANA

London and New York

First published in 1985
Reprinted 1986 and 1987
by ARKANA, an imprint of Routledge & Kegan Paul Ltd
11 New Fetter Lane,
London EC4P 4EE

Published in the U.S.A. by
Routledge and Kegan Paul Inc.
in association with Methuen Inc.
29 West 35th Street, New York,
NY 10001

Set in Sabon, 10 on 11pt
by Ann Buchan (Typesetters)
and printed in the British Isles
by Guernsey Press Co. Ltd,
Guernsey, Channel Islands

Library of Congress Cataloguing in Publication Data

Grey, Margot.

Return from death.
Bibliography: p.
Includes index.
1. Astral projection.   2. Death, Apparent.
I. Title.
BF1389.A7G74      1985       133.9'01'3      85-1428

ISBN 1-85063-019-4

For Nona Coxhead

whose efforts to promote my research
prompted the writing of this book

# *Contents*

# Foreword

When, during the summer of 1984, I had the opportunity to spend some time with Margot Grey in London, I soon found myself in a state of bemused, but excited, astonishment. My odd condition, however, had an ordinary cause: a simple book exchange. Here's the story:

Just before arriving in England, my latest book on the near-death experience (NDE), *Heading Toward Omega,* had been published in the United States. Naturally, knowing I would be seeing Margot, I tucked a copy in my suitcase for her and, once we had had a chance to chat, I presented the book to her. Margot thanked me and quickly indicated that she meant to return the favor – she had a manuscript for me, and she wanted me to read it during my stay.

Now Margot and I had actually met several years before, in 1981, when she came to the International Association for Near-Death Studies, which I then headed, at the University of Connecticut, in order to begin her own comparative study of the NDE. She stayed with us for two weeks at that time and endeared herself to everyone on our staff with her lively enthusiasm, captivating conversation and her already deep understanding of near-death phenomena. As a result of her 'internship' with us, Margot and I became good friends and promised to keep in touch once she returned to England.

And so we did – after a fashion, but, since we both continued to be very busy, our fashion was to write very occasional hasty notes, promising a 'real letter' when we found the (non-existent) leisure to write one. Not surprisingly, then, there was more warmth and good wishes in our correspondence than there was content. I knew that Margot was writing a thesis on NDEs – in due course I received a copy of it – but of Margot's larger writing projects I remained ignorant. In my own case, my life during the years that spanned our visits was primarily consumed with my new research into the aftermath and meaning of the NDE which culminated in my own book. Nevertheless, as many authors tend to be, I was fairly closed-mouth about my 'work in progress'; consequently, Margot herself knew virtually nothing about its substance or conclusions.

Thus, when we finally exchanged books in London, it was without any real knowledge of what the other had been up to. Of course, I was eager to find out, so while Margot busied herself with dinner preparations for the company she had invited for that evening's gathering, I betook myself up to her study to begin reading her manuscript. It was there that I gradually became extremely agitated, even shocked, by what I read.

You see, Margot had somehow contrived to write, entirely independently of my own research during the past three years, her own version of *Heading Toward Omega*! I could scarcely believe what I was reading in Margot's book – precisely because it was so close to what I had put into mine. I could scarcely remain in Margot's study either because I would keep finding myself dashing down the stairs into the kitchen saying, 'Margot, I just can't get over your book . . .', etc., and generally carrying on in ways that no cook can countenance for very long. Finally, I was forced to retreat to her study and read on until the last guest had arrived and the evening's social obligations won out over my preferences.

Now, you may be – and I hope you are – wondering just what it was in Margot's book that so compelled my interest and what, I trust, will command yours. Let me tell you – and in this give you a bit of preview of the book itself as well as a sense of its significance for the general reader.

In the first part of her book, Margot means to give a general summary of what we know about what these days is called 'the near-death experience', in short, what people *experience* when they are for a moment on the threshold of death or when they pass into a temporary state of clinical death. Most of the research into this phenomenon prior to Margot's book was conducted in the United States. In this book, however, Margot presents the findings from her own study – the first such investigation carried out in the UK – which allows the reader to determine the extent to which NDEs here parallel those in the US. For those not yet more than superficially familiar with this phenomenon, this part of the book will be very powerful indeed, for NDEs are experiences of extraordinary compellingness and obvious spiritual import. Readers already acquainted with NDEs will find the material offered here to be a satisfying account of what is known about NDEs – and will find some intriguing new discoveries as well that deserve more attention than they have as yet received from researchers.

It is in the second half of this volume, however, that new ground is broken for all readers since it is here that Margot begins to explore the after-effects of NDEs and their larger meanings – and it is chiefly here that Margot has essentially and *independently* duplicated the main findings and conclusions of *Heading Toward Omega*. In these chapters, she delineates the changes in values and outlook reported by NDErs following their close brush with death; the paranormal phenomena they experience afterward, some of which have very sobering but ultimately hopeful significance; the development of the gift of healing that some NDErs display; and the possible evolutionary implications of the NDE itself. I will not deprive the reader of the intellectual and emotional satisfaction to be derived from this part of the book by divulging the general *pattern* that Margot's own research discloses and which she explicates in any case with great clarity. Suffice it to say that the evidence she adduces in support of her overall thesis replicates mine, and her conclusions likewise coincide with my own.

I emphasise this concordance between our separate books, not simply out of a sense either of immodesty or delight or even of relief that another investigator has corroborated one's own findings, but for another reason altogether. Quite frankly, as critics may be quick to point out, Margot's research is based on a small sample of NDErs and though some statistical information is presented in *Return from Death*, her study is clearly only a first step toward the kind of scientific research that Margot's book is designed to stimulate. For that reason, some readers might feel that Margot's conclusions outstrip her own data and are therefore unwarranted generalisations. While this *may* be so, I would urge readers to be aware that others, such as myself, have indeed discerned the same patterns in our own data and that, consequently, Margot's conclusions *are* buttressed by additional findings she did not know of when she was writing this book. To be sure, my own research is subject to methodological criticisms (whose isn't?), but that very research has at least been helpful to me in allowing me to appreciate the argument that Margot makes in her book even when her own data might appear too frail fully to support it.

Make no mistake about it: *Return from Death* is a most important book. If Margot Grey's reading of the significance of NDEs is at all accurate, then this book contains not only a hint about the life to come after death, but, perhaps of more immediate concern to many of us, it conveys an inspiring promise of the collective life to come *on earth* and, if Margot's views are well-founded, it gives us a shining picture of the spiritual evolution of humanity – which is manifesting *now*.

Kenneth Ring, PhD

# Preface

In February 1976, while travelling through India, I was struck down by a strange illness which was never conclusively diagnosed. During the three week period that it lasted I hovered on the brink of death, while my temperature soared to 105 degrees. At some point during the process of passing in and out of consciousness I became aware that if I somehow urged myself I could rise up out of my body and remain in a state of levitation up against the ceiling in a corner of the room. At the time this seemed entirely natural and felt very pleasant and extremely freeing. I remember looking down at my body lying on the bed and feeling completely unperturbed by the fact that it seemed likely that I was going to die in a strange country half a world away from home, family and friends, and thinking it was really totally unimportant where I left my body, which I felt had served me well and like a favourite but worn out coat had at last outlived its usefulness and would now have to be discarded.

At one point during the early part of my illness I remember finding myself floating in total darkness in what seemed to be outer space. It was like being in or part of absolutely nothing. I recall thinking, 'So this is what happens when one dies, it's just absolute nothingness, just black limitless space', and yet I was not afraid of it nor did I feel lonely. I was conscious of my own identity and aware of my aloneness, yet at the same time I found myself to be 'one' with infinite space; I seemed to be part of it and it was part of me.

Later on, I seemed to be travelling down an endless tunnel. I could see a pin-point of light at the end of the tunnel towards which I seemed to be moving and which was gradually drawing nearer. I remember knowing with absolute certainty that I would eventually be through the tunnel and would emerge into the light, which was like the light of a very bright star but much more brilliant. A sense of exultation was accompanied by a feeling of

xiii

being very close to the 'source' of life and love, which seemed to be
one. I felt embraced by such feelings of bliss, that there are no
words to describe the feeling. The nearest I can come to it in
human terms is to recall the rapture of being 'in love', the emotion
one feels when one's first born is put into one's arms for the first
time, the transcendence of spirit that can sometimes occur when
one is at a concert of classical music, the peace and grandeur of
mountains, forests and lakes or other beauties of nature that can
move one to tears of joy. Unite all these together and magnify a
thousand times and you get a glimpse of the 'state of being' that
one is in when the restriction to one's 'true heritage' is partially
removed. I think this is what the injunction 'Be ye perfect, even as
your Father in Heaven is perfect' must mean.

On returning to England, having recovered sufficiently to make
the homeward journey, I realised something very significant had
occurred which I can only compare to a spiritual rebirth. My
mental energies seemed extended and refined by a new
consciousness and I determined to study the phenomena that I had
experienced in order to try to discover what other people
experienced when apparently on the threshold of imminent death.

# Acknowledgments

When, shortly after completing my comparative study of NDEs, I was approached by Eileen Wood at Routledge & Kegan Paul and asked if I would be willing to write a book about my research, I enthusiastically accepted the challenge. The actual production was altogether another matter.

For helping me to complete this task, my thanks are due to Hugh Drake, not only for his unfailing support and encouragement, but for reading the entire text, as I went along, and suggesting many improvements. To Ray Atkin, who also read the text and urged me on when my confidence needed bolstering, I am also grateful. And to Liz Towner, my appreciation for her valuable feedback and for typing the manuscript so beautifully, even though it sometimes meant putting in long hours to get it finished on time.

My thanks are also due to Dr Raghu Gaind, for kindly allowing me to take study leave from the course I am currently engaged in with the Institute of Social Psychiatry at Guy's Hospital, to allow me to devote more time and energy to the work.

I am most grateful to Dr Peter Nixon, for his assistance and co-operation in allowing me to interview a number of his patients. I also owe a debt of gratitude to Dr Peter Fenwick, for his help in explaining the neurological processes involved in mystical experience.

A very special thank-you goes to Kenneth Ring, whose boundless generosity in sharing his research methodology and his home with me, at a time when I was struggling to get started, was the spur I needed to put together my research project.

I am further indebted to John Rowan, for taking time to discuss the ideas in this book and for reading the manuscript and making many helpful suggestions. Also to Anita Gregory, for her valuable advice and generous assistance in correcting the final manuscript and pointing out various ways of improving the text.

To Nona Coxhead my thanks for suggesting the title and for reading and commenting on corrections to the finished text; and to Eileen Wood, my editor, for her guiding hand on my manuscript.

To the many people too numerous to name, who have directly or indirectly contributed to the ideas in this work, I wish to express my sincere appreciation.

In acknowledging my debts, I am aware of the enormous obligation owed to my brother for the use of his beach-side flat in which to spread myself and work undisturbed, and my deep gratitude for his understanding and co-operation during his spells of home leave.

Finally, my thanks go out to all those near-death survivors whose willingness to share their experiences made the publication of this book possible.

# PART 1

# *Approaching Death*

# CHAPTER 1

# *Introduction: Towards an understanding of near-death phenomena*

That which we call death, is but the other side of life.
*Ramacharaka*

Death is something that affects us all, for it is an integral part of life. From the moment of birth it is certain that we will eventually die, it is only a question of when. But, although there are few situations in human life, apart from birth, that can equal the significance of dying and death, in modern times the subject has been treated with disgust by western civilisation with its materialistic approach to life emphasising achievement and success, and death has in consequence been generally evaded, ignored and denied.

In Freud's day sex was the taboo subject, but today it is death. For to die is perceived as having failed in the game of lifemanship, and this attitude is largely confirmed by the current medical approach to a dying person, which is governed by a determined effort to overcome death or at least to delay its arrival by every possible means: another disease to be conquered; the 'last enemy to be destroyed' in this materialistic, technological age.

Today, however, when we are faced by death and destruction on a scale never before imagined by mankind, it is essential that we study the subject of death in order to learn the lessons that are contained within it. For those who seek to understand death's meaning come to recognise that death is a transformative process and that the highest spiritual values of life can originate from the contemplation and examination of death. Furthermore, it seems likely that the key to the mystery of death is also the one that unlocks the door of life.

3

This question of death's meaning has been known to concern human beings ever since recorded history, and philosophers of all ages have pondered its mysteries seeking to find an answer. It is a riddle of human existence that has preoccupied mankind down the centuries in an attempt to solve its enigma, so that the apparent finality of death can be unmasked and robbed of its strangeness and terror. For it appears that until we are able to clarify the meaning of death we seem destined never fully to understand the signficance of life.

The idea that life continues in some form or another after death is central to almost every major religious tradition throughout the world. For although the concept of life after death may vary with different cultures and ideologies, basically what they all seem to be saying is that death is not the end of existence, and that consciousness continues in a different form after the body is no longer vital.

However, although up to now we have mostly had to accept this belief in a life hereafter on trust, there have nevertheless always been a number of saintly men and women in every age who claimed to have had a direct experience of God or some source of universal life and love. As a result of their encounter these people were subsequently convinced that consciousness is not dependent on a physical body, and that once the mind is free of its sensory restriction it is able to experience other realities. These exceptional human beings who down the ages were first-hand recipients of this knowledge no longer needed to have faith in God and a life after death, as from henceforward they KNEW with certainty that God existed and that life continued after death.

In recent times a similar phenomenon has been reported by hundreds of ordinary men and women with no particular religious or spiritual aspirations, and often with no prior knowledge of metaphysical or esoteric phenomena. This experience, remarkable in its impact and of great contemporary significance, puts into question the whole proposition of what is assumed to take place at the time of death. It has come to be known as the Near-Death Experience (NDE).

It has been recorded since the dawn of history that the onset of death can bring about profound changes in consciousness, and descriptions of the experiences of people who almost died during the course of severe illness or injury, or who were believed to be dead but were subsequently resuscitated or revived, have been confirmed down the centuries. Indeed NDEs have been alluded to by philosophers and mystics since time immemorial. The historical accounts of people who have attested to the experience as being one of transcendent reality are manifold, and the revelatory quality of these experiences has inspired many an ancient philosopher such as Pythagoras as well as modern writers like Walt Whitman. However, it is only recently that psychologists have seriously concerned themselves with the study of what people report experiencing when apparently approaching the threshold of death.

With the emergence of the new areas of consciousness research, however, investigation of NDEs has recently developed into a serious field of study. This has, furthermore, been encouraged by the advances in modern resuscitation techniques which have increased the number of people alive today who have nearly died or have undergone 'clinical death'. As the ranks of these people who were brought back from the gates of death multiplied, a growing number reported that during the period when there was complete cessation of vital signs of life, extraordinary phenomena occurred which defied their accepted ideas of what happens when death occurs. Nevertheless, the challenge to examine this phenomenon has until recently been largely ignored, as the medical and religious reaction to the experience seems generally to have been a denial of the possibility of its existence and its consequent dismissal: 'It can't be true, therefore it isn't true.' Could it be, as has been suggested, that the reason behind the reluctance of many members of the helping professions to get involved with the psychological issues surrounding the dying period is due to their own unresolved fears of biological impermanence and death?

There is, however, one notable exception – the distinguished Swiss-born American psychiatrist Elisabeth Kübler-Ross, a remarkable woman of great courage who is acknowledged to be one of the world's most renowned thanatologists, specialising in the study of death in all its aspects, and known across the globe for her pioneering work with dying patients. During the course of her career she has become convinced that when a person is on the verge of imminent death, something very unusual seems to occur, and since she first drew attention to it, about a decade ago, a revival of interest has been generated in NDEs which has led to a growing number of studies based on systematic research being initiated.

These experiences, which are characterised by a common pattern, include such elements as an overwhelming feeling of peace and well-being, finding oneself out of one's body, floating or being propelled through a dark void, becoming aware of a brilliant white or golden lightn encountering and communicating with a 'presence' or 'being of light', at which time one's fate is generally decided, seeing a panoramic review of one's life, entering a world of supernal beauty and recognising deceased loved ones and conversing with them, and a number of other transcendental elements. The phenomenon usually has a pro-found effect on the person who has experienced it, not the least of which is a greatly diminished fear of death.

Although the existence of NDEs has now been thoroughly established in America with the publication of a number of substantial research studies, which have noted and duly recorded the specific elements encountered within the near-death episode, certain questions nevertheless remain unanswered. For instance: would the same components be met with in near-death episodes in other countries? With the exception of a study carried out by two parapsychologists, Karlis Osis and Erlendur Haraldsson, entitled *At the Hour of Death* which was designed to examine the deathbed visions and mood changes of dying people in both America and India, I know of no other study that has set out specifically to investigate this cross-cultural aspect. While I felt sure that a British study would prove to be materially similar to the ones undertaken in America, it was none the less necessary for research to be carried out in order to establish this point empirically.

So, starting early in 1981, I began my own search for people who had come close to death as a result of illness, accident or suicide attempt and who, in some instances, had even suffered a 'clinical death', which involved the loss of all vital signs of life such as heartbeat and respiration. Encouraged by the inquiry into the new area of consciousness research that was being developed in America, and which was moving away from the old restrictions, I set about looking to see what investigations into NDEs I could find that were currently taking place in Britain. As I could find none I decided to initiate research into this field of study myself. One of the first questions that I determined to find an answer to was whether the pattern of NDEs in a life threatening situation would prove to be essentially the same in Britain as those discerned by researchers in America, or if the subject matter reported would prove to be in any way different from that so far described. If so, to what extent, I wondered, would differing cultural characteristics affect the experiences so far related? And what would the after-effects reveal? Would the impact of coming so close to death have the same profound effect and alter the lives of the individuals concerned in the same significant way as had been reported in the American surveys?

From the works written on the subject to date, the impression I gained is that one of the noteworthy aspects of the experience is that it appears to be universal and seems to differ little from one person to another regardless of race, cultural background, religious persuasion or social standing. The most common pattern that emerges is one of inexpressible beauty, peace and ultimate transcendence. The after-effects of this experience seem generally to be the same for most respondents: the fear of death tends to be greatly reduced and they become more loving, compassionate and less materially orientated. The impact is described as being akin to a spiritual rebirth.

This had certainly proved to be the case in my own instance, so that I am aware of being influenced by both personal and professional factors in designing a research project to examine whether these experiences had more universal validity. But although I have attempted to pursue my study in a scientific manner, and to provide statistical data wherever this seemed appropriate and useful, I am well aware of the fact that there comes a point at which a limit to scientific interpretation is reached. I doubt whether in the final analysis death will ever yield its ultimate secrets to the impersonal probing of scientific investigation.

In referring to this dilemma, Carl Rogers has aptly stated:

I am not at all disturbed by those who say 'but this is not science!' When studies are unbiased, communicable and replicable, they are science, and I have confidence that we could learn more significantly about human mysteries if we whole-heartedly enlisted the intelligence and insight of the person involved.

It is my belief that a willingness to be open to new paradigms, and an attitude which allows an unbiased approach to matters concerning the value of life and death, more readily lend themselves to the possiblility of an understanding of the human mysteries. By being prepared to accept unconditionally the impressions of the people involved in any situation, it allows their experience to speak and so aids the process by which one may be afforded the opportunity of finding answers to the perennial questions concerning the riddles of existence.

George Gallup Jnr, who is probably best known for his internationally operating Gallup Poll organisation, recently published a survey of the near-death experience entitled *Adventures in Immortality*, in which he suggests:

> In some ways psychiatrists, psychologists and those in related disciplines may be in an even better position than physical scientists and theologians to evaluate some of these close brushes with death. They, more than professionals in any other discipline, are constantly probing the frontiers of unusual mental activity in their daily work. Also, those in the mental health field are doing some of the most creative research to unveil the meaning of the near-death encounter.

It is a willingness to risk deviating from the rule that has always proved historically to be one of the greatest incentives to the advancement of human understanding, for what appear to be new phenomena may in fact actually be true anomalies that our previous beliefs were unable to encounter. The freedom to explore new perspectives afforded by a more liberal psychology allows an unhampered approach, and it is from this viewpoint that my proposition will be examined.

This approach has been amply demonstrated by Elisabeth Kübler-Ross whose work has to a very large extent stimulated the recent revival of interest in death-related phenomena. She saw that the final stages of life with all the attendant anxieties, fears and hopes could in actual fact be a time of learning and growth, and recognising that it was important to acknowledge the new and challenging opportunities and to refocus on the human aspects of the death process in order to learn about the functioning of the human mind, so as to understand the unique changes that can occur in the human psyche at this time.

Before reporting on the results of my study, I feel it is appropriate to look first at this new awareness of the psychological needs of the terminally ill that have developed out of the pioneering work of Dr Kübler-Ross, in order to try to discover what lessons are inherent in the journey towards death for the living as well as for the dying. For it was out of this work that her observations of the phenomenon that we will be examining arose.

Today, at the same time as attempts to prolong life with organ transplants and life support machinery continue to advance, people, especially older people, are finding themselves becoming ever more isolated and alone as their numbers rise. The result is that there now exists an ever-increasing number of people with malignant and chronic disorders, together with the psychosomatic and emotional problems that have resulted from social changes that have taken place in the last few decades. This revolution has ultimately been responsible for an increased fear of dying, due to unfamiliarity with the processes of nature, which has affected birth as well as death. By dehumanising the experience, people have been removed from participating in the actual event, thereby causing a splitting off of the psychic involvement, which in turn has given rise to the current need for greater understanding to be applied to coping with the problems of dying and death that have arisen as a result of this state of affairs. In her book *On Death and Dying*, Dr Kübler-Ross points out:

> We would think that our great emancipation, our knowledge of science and of man, had given us better ways and means to prepare ourselves and our families for this inevitable happening. Instead the days are gone when a man was allowed to die in peace and dignity in his own home.

It seems that the more advances we are making in science, the more death is feared and its actuality denied. This flight from reality appears to be due to the fact that nowadays dying is in many ways becoming more gruesome as it becomes more mechanical. It has even become increasingly difficult recently to determine the technical moment when death actually occurs and many thanatologists, particularly in America, have been challenging and amending the legal criteria for death. For now that the advances in medical science make it possible to sustain some 'vital signs', such as breathing and heartbeat, while other signs, such as brainwaves, are absent, where is the line to be drawn? Is a person whose heart beats and whose lungs draw breath alive if the brain is dead? In a life-threatening situation in an emergency ward, however, there is obviously no time in which to debate decisions which must be decisively made during the crisis period, regarding whether either to pronounce the patient dead or to continue life-support systems. Nevertheless, it seems that the legal consequences of some of these decisions will continue to be a subject for exploraton in the law courts for a long time to come.

Meanwhile, dying becomes more lonely and impersonal as patients are more frequently being taken out of their familiar environment and rushed to emergency wards. This journey to the hospital is often the first episode in the dying process. While it cannot be denied that many lives are saved by the timely intervention of hospitalisation, it is nevertheless both necessary and relevant that the focus on the individuals' experience, as well as on their needs and reactions, be maintained. All too often, severely ill patients are denied any right to an opinion of their own. Decisions regarding whether they should be hospitalised and if so, when and where, are often made by others. If at this point people raise too many objections, they will in all probability be sedated (for their own good!) and if the case is sufficiently interesting it may even become an object of great concern and financial investment.

The desire to be allowed to die in peace will be met with 'infusions, transfusions, a heart machine, or a tracheotomy', as Dr Kübler-Ross has observed. Instead of a comforting hand to hold or an encouraging word, individuals in this situation will instead, more often than not, have people 'busily preoccupied with their heart rate, pulse, electrocardiogram or pulmonary functions, secretions or excretions'; everything, in fact, except their needs as human beings. Any attempt to fight against this will be futile since all this is being done in the fight to prolong their life. A person cannot be considered when his or her life is at stake. Dr Kübler-Ross has rightly inquired:

Is the reason for this increasingly mechanical, depersonal-
ised approach our own defensiveness? Is this approach our
own way to cope with and repress the anxieties that a
terminally or critically ill patient evokes in us? Is our
concentration on equipment, on blood pressure, our
desperate attempt to deny the impending end, which is so
frightening and discomforting to us that we displace all our
knowledge onto machines, since they are less close to us
than the suffering face of another human being which would
remind us once more of our lack of omnipotence, our own
limitations and fallibility and, last but not least perhaps, our
own mortality?

Whatever the answer may be, while at a physical level there is less
suffering, the price we seem to be paying for this is in the
ever-increasing level of emotional pain that continues to rise as a
result of this intensified dehumanisation.

It was her observation of these painful feelings which surface
when people are confronted by dying and death that prompted Dr
Kübler-Ross to chart the stages of emotional response through
which terminally ill patients pass, and it is largely due to her
efforts that today's new awareness of the individual's need for
compassion and personal attention in the final stages of life have
become recognised. She was the first to draw both public and
professional attention to the psychological mechanisms involved
which enable people to find ways of coping in the face of death.

# CHAPTER 2
# *Near-death studies:*
# *a contemporary review*

No man can reveal to you aught but that which
already lies half asleep in the dawning of your
knowledge

*Kahlil Gibran*

Attention was first drawn to the near-death experience in the early
1970s by Dr Kubler-Ross, who had begun to observe the
phenomenon while engaged in her pioneering study of examining
what people were experiencing during the process of dying. Her
reputation, which had been rapidly growing as a result of her
controversial work with dying patients, was equalled by her
increasing popularity arising from her public appearances, so that
when she began to talk openly about NDEs her remarks caused a
considerable stir. At the time she claimed to have interviewed
hundreds (now thousands) of patients who had reported NDEs,
and her revelations have probably done more to alert both public
and professional awareness of this phenomenon than those of any
ther single person, despite the fact that to date she has never
published any systematic account of her findings.

The general response to the comments about NDEs made by Dr
Kübler-Ross was amazingly positive and this undoubtedly helps
to explain the extraordinary success that greeted the publication
in 1975 of a book about NDEs that came out just at a time when
Dr Kübler-Ross was considering putting her own research
findings on paper. The book entitled *Life After Life*, which was
written by Raymond Moody, an American psychiatrist, delineated the prototype NDE (a term he coined), in which he described
the results of eleven years of research into NDEs, based on about
150 cases. The world-wide popularity of the book was
astonishing and may well have enabled more people on an
international scale to understand what can occur when death is

12

imminent than any other written on the subject to date. On the whole, the findings of Dr Kübler-Ross and Moody were in agreement with each other and generally tended to support the 'survival view' of the phenomenon which had been advanced by parapsychologists.

While great prominence has been given to the near-death phenomenon as a result of the attention it has received arising from the work of Kübler-Ross and Moody, it would nevertheless be a considerable oversight to disregard the fact that research into the evidence for survival after death had been going on for almost a century prior to its recent publicity. Much careful and scholarly work was done in those early days by the founders and early members of he British and American Societies for Psychical Research, but it was not until modern techniques of resuscitation made available NDEs in sufficient numbers that significant empirical progress was possible.

Among the modern American parapsychologists who have undertaken research of death-related phenomena, possibly the most renowned is Karlis Osis. His now widely known investigation, first published in 1961 by the Parapsychological Foundation under the title 'Deathbed Observations by Physicians and Nurses', examined the phenomenological features and mood changes associated with the visions of dying patients as reported by hospital staff. Then, in 1977, Osis together with Erlendur Haraldsson, an Icelandic colleague, published a book entitled *At the Hour of Death*, in which they described research they had undertaken in both America and India. Their cross-cultural study set out to examine the experiential aspects associated with the deathbed visions of the dying individuals in both countries and resulted in their finding considerable phenomenological similarities. These death-related experiences refer only to certain aspects of NDEs, however, and were often described by witnesses to the event many years after the incident and were seldom obtained from the experiencers themselves. Therefore, while their studies make a valuable contribution to 'survival research', they do not really qualify for inclusion within the category of genuine NDE research *per se*.

Probably the first actual near-death study as such in recent times, and the one which proved to be the forerunner of today's near-death research, was the investigation that was undertaken by

Professor Albert Heim during the last century. A Swiss geologist by profession, Heim spent many years collecting accounts of the experiences of people who had been involved in mountain climbing accidents. He was himself an enthusiastic mountain climber who had on a number of occasions experienced near-fatal falls, and as a result was apparently the first known person to have collected the experiences of other people to whom similar misadventures had befallen. During the last twenty-five years of his life he interviewed many individuals who had come close to death through accidents of various kinds, including warfare, but his main interest seems always to have been accidental falls.

Heim's record of his life's work lay forgotten, until it was uncovered by the psychiatrist Russell Noyes Jnr, who together with a colleague, Ray Kletti, published a translation of his work in the early 1970s. This study, it seems, was the inspiration for further research undertaken by Noyes and Kletti; while continuing in the same tradition as Heim, their work further supported and enlarged upon the information that was contained in the original account. As Professor Kenneth Ring, founder of the International Association for Near-Death Studies (IANDS), has pointed out, Noyes' work was of great significance in that he was the first physician to investigate the near-death phenomenon, thus shifting the emphasis from the realms of parapsychology to that of medicine. He was also the first to study the experiences of dying individuals by directly interviewing near-death survivors, thereby setting a trend that has continued to characterise near-death studies ever since. His work with Kletti, which continued to emphasise the experiences of impending accidental death, proposed a 'depersonalisation' theory in response to the stress of imminent death. This is seen as an ego-defence mechanism which protects the individual against the unbearable prospect of approaching death, so that the resultant feeling of detachment and transcendence has the effect of desensitising the insupportable impact of their expected near-death crisis.

The interest stimulated in the subject by the pioneering work of Kübler-Ross, Moody and Noyes had the effect of encouraging a number of other enterprising American psychologists to study the phenomenon in order to further explore the preliminary observations that had been made thus far. Prominent among these is Kenneth Ring, who is Professor of Psychology at the University of Connecticut in America. His book entitled *Life at Death*, published in 1980, was the first reported scientific investigation of NDEs. This study, based on over a hundred interviews with near-death survivors, includes statistical analysis of his data, backed up by extensive quantitive material. Aimed at comparing NDEs of illness, accident and suicide attempt survivors, *Life at Death* showed that the NDE was largely invariant over different conditions of near-death onset, and also revealed that there was a high incidence of occurrence in all the categories that he studied.

Dr Ring has stated that his own interest in the investigation of NDEs has always been motivated by a desire to put the study of the phenomenon on a more scientific basis, so that with 'sound research on which to base their evaluations', members of the scientific and medical community would be encouraged to give the subject their serious consideration. He further pointed out that 'a plethora of anecdotal books on the topic' had already stimulated a great deal of interest in the experience, but had so far failed to answer many basic questions which his book sets out to rectify.

Coming from a background in transpersonal psychology and with a special interest in altered states of consciousness, Ring was already familiar with NDEs before Moody's work was published, but his curiosity was evidently still further aroused by reading *Life After Life*, so that while he 'didn't really question the basic model' described in the book, it was the unanswered questions that seem to have prompted his investigation of the phenomenon.

Furthermore, he followed his initial inquiry into the subject with the formation of the International Association for Near-Death Studies, which is dedicated to the exploration of NDEs and the implications inherent in the experience. With the founding of this organisation he has encouraged investigation of this phenomenon to be carried out on an international scale and has raised the standard of research to a scientific level. His promotion of near-death studies has undoubtedly made a lasting contribution to the understanding of a phenomenon that is of great relevance today, and will certainly bring comfort and hope to many people. For not only will those who have had a NDE find that they are not alone, but they will also find encouragement to explore the innate potential for self-realisation that is contained within the experience. It is further to be hoped that the helping professions, whose work involves caring for the dying and comforting the bereaved, will be encouraged to examine the work done in the field so far, in order that they may be aided in their own task. For, as conscious awareness of the phenomenon gradually enlarges the scope of human understanding, so hopefully a more compassionate approach to the psychic issues involved in the experience of near-death episodes will evolve, reducing the fear of ridicule and the feelings of isolation and loneliness that many of these individuals are obliged to endure.

About the same time as Dr Ring was engaged in conducting his research and establishing IANDS, another major study of NDEs was being undertaken by Michael Sabom, a cardiologist who is Assistant Professor of Medicine at Emory University School of Medicine. His book, *Recollections of Death*, published early in 1982, reports the results of interviews with 116 near-death survivors. Unlike Ring, who seems to have basically accepted the possibility of NDEs before embarking on his own research, Sabom's position was apparently quite the contrary. He evidently started out with the conviction that there was 'no such thing as inexplicable phenomena', that all the so-called mysteries were in reality 'scientific facts' awaiting discovery, and that providing the proper scientific methodology was applied most, if not all, of the 'unanswered questions of the universe would eventually be answered in one form or another'.

It was apparently with a certain amount of scepticism, therefore, that he was persuaded to participate in a programme about NDEs which a colleague, Sarah Kreutziger, had agreed to arrange. The idea was that the presentation would be based on a discussion of the material contained in Moody's book *Life After Life*, which was Sabom's first introduction to the work. As a result, it was decided that they would conduct a brief survey of their own hospitalised patients who had survived a near-death crisis similar to those under discussion, in order to add substance to the presentation. It was his amazement at finding that the patients' answers to his questions matched the description in Moody's survey that prompted Sabom to undertake his own 'scientific study' with the aid of Kreutziger.

While his overall findings are in accord with Ring's study, Sabom's book is distinguished by the care that he took to provide independent corroborative evidence for the visual and auditory perceptions reported by near-death survivors when allegedly out of the body, so that his research data strongly support the claims made by his respondents. He also gives special attention to medical interpretations of NDEs and concludes that none of those so far proposed is adequate to account for NDEs as a whole; in this he concurs with Ring.

Although there have been a number of additional empirical studies of near-death phenomena in America undertaken from the perspective of several other disciplines which also emphasise the positive view of the incident, there are only two more surveys that I want to mention briefly at this point, since they include an aspect of the experience that other studies to date have generally failed to identify. I refer to what is sometimes felt to be a negative experience.

The first to draw attention to this aspect of the phenomenon was Maurice Rawlings, a cardiologist working in Chattanooga, Tennessee. According to his own account, Rawlings, like Sabom, started out by regarding the so-called 'after death' experiences that were being rumoured at the time as 'fantasy or conjecture or imagination'. It seems that the turning point in his thinking came one evening in 1977 when he was resuscitating a 'terrified patient' who reported upon recovery that he had been in hell. Rawlings states that he was used to working with patients who were under extreme emotional stress, but he seems to have been struck by something in this particular individual's manner which impressed him as being outside the usual expression of fear. He noticed that 'he had a grotesque grimace expressing sheer horror! His pupils were dilated, and he was perspiring and trembling – he looked as if his hair was "on end". He pleaded desperately: "Don't stop. . . . Don't let me go back to hell!" ' As most patients upon recovering consciousness following a cardiac arrest usually asked for the external heart massage to be stopped, as it can be quite rough, this seemed like a very unusual request. By now Rawlings seems to have become so alarmed by his patient's plea that he started to work with 'feverish' speed and it was evidently only after 'the patient had experienced three or four episodes of complete unconsciousness and clinical death from cessation of both heartbeat and breathing' that his condition became stable. At some point between passing in and out of consciousness during the course of these near-death episodes he asked, 'How do I stay out of hell?' As Rawlings naturally did not know the answer, he could only suggest that perhaps the solution might lie in prayer, though at the time it appears that he did not have much faith in the power of prayer. For having, as he puts it, 'always dealt with death as a routine occurrence in my medical practice, regarding it as an extinction', he had never up to that time given much thought to 'this life after death business', or to the possibility that there might be someone who would be able to respond to one's entreaties.

However, the episode just related seems to have had such an unnerving effect on himthat he decided to start investigating the phenomenon further. So, two days after the events described, Dr Rawlings approached his patient with the intention of obtaining a more detailed account of what had actually happened during the time he purported to have been in 'hell'. To his utter astonishment his patient was unable to recall any unpleasant incident. From this he concluded that the events experienced at the time must have been so frightening and terrible that his patient's 'conscious mind could not cope with them and they were subsequently suppressed far into his sub-conscious'. The main hypothesis of Rawlings' research, published in 1978 under the title *Beyond Death's Door*, proposes that the absence of any hellish experiences reported in the other studies up to that time is due to the fact that the information was mostly obtained some time after the event took place. He points out that as a cardiologist, whose speciality is resuscitation, he is usually able to be present at the scene of a near-death episode so that he is in a better position than most to observe as well as to interview the patient immediately afterwards. He further draws attention to the fact that the patient whose experience has just been cited was only able to recall the positive elements of his experience, such as being in 'a gorge full of beautiful colours', while out of his body, when questioned later. His findings therefore suggest that the apparently selective recall might operate in a similar way to the dynamic interpretation proposed by Noyes and Kletti, whereby the ego-defence mechanism protects the individual from having to face an unbearable situation.

The other study that acknowledges the existence of negative experiences is the recently published *Adventures in Immortality*. Written by George Gallup Jnr, this investigation, conducted over eighteen months, was carried out with the full resources of the internationally known Gallup Poll Organisation and covered the whole of America. His findings suggest that the incidence of NDEs among Americans is in fact much more prevalent than had been hitherto suggested, which bears out Dr Kübler-Ross's contention. As Kenneth Ring has observed, the importance of Gallup's book is that it conclusively establishes the extensiveness and authenticity of NDEs. For, by conducting a survey based on the most rigorous sampling procedures, his renowned organisation has provided data based on a very substantial quantity of demographic information, which supports the conclusions reached by researchers to date, but which for the most part have been based on small and non-representative samples.

Starting with an examination of people's beliefs in life after death, the survey then goes on to explore what those people who had been in a near-death situation had experienced.Of special interest to us here is the chapter entitled 'Descent into the Abyss', which gives us an idea of what the contents might include. He starts off by suggesting that people generally assume that when they die they will automatically move into some sort of union with God or 'Ultimate Reality', that any other state of continuing existence is unthinkable. He then goes on to propose:

> But just as there is good and evil on earth, so the nagging suspicion persists that some aspects of the afterlife, for whatever reason, may not be so nice. To put it in its crassest terms, what about the abyss, the inferno, the eternal death or estrangement from God – what about hell?

To find out the answer, in 1952, 1965 and 1981, a national sample of adult Americans were asked, 'Do you think there is a Hell, to which people who have led bad lives and die without being sorry are eternally damned?' The results of this question, which proved to be strikingly consistent, were 'yes' in 58 per cent, 54 per cent and 53 per cent respectively over the years. Even so, Gallup reveals that these figures are nevertheless considerably lower than the corresponding seven out of ten who consistently said that they believed in heaven in those same years.

He further points out that an interesting fact that emerged from the special survey undertaken for his book concerned the background of those people who did or didn't believe in hell. He found that those from the South tended to have the strongest beliefs in Hell, with a 72 per cent affirmation, going up even higher in the Deep South, with an 81 per cent endorsement, as opposed to 36 per cent in the West and 41 per cent in the East. One is tempted to speculate whether this could be a factor which might possibly account for the discrepancy between the findings of Rawlings and the other studies referred to which all emphasise the notable absence of any hellish elements.

Although only one per cent of NDEs reported a hell-like experience in Gallup's national poll, he suggests that these figures are in reality more complex than they would at first sight appear to be. He argues that among the 'relatively large number' of people who indicated that they hadn't experienced heaven during their close brush with death, it also seemed clear that many of these people had either a neutral or negative experience that caused them to exclude the presence of God or some heavenly dimension in their evaluations of the incident. At any rate, they were reluctant to interpret their experience in positive terms. He goes on to conclude:

> We know that the large majority of near-death experiences have been described in neutral or negative terms, but does this necessarily mean they involved hell?
>
> Certainly most of our respondents – and that includes more than six in ten people in our survey who reported coming close to death – merely described their accident or serious illness, without injecting mystical elements into their account. Also, the negative descriptions and evaluations of the near-death experiences were often only mildly negative; or in some cases, they mixed negative and positive elements together.
>
> This scenario may not be quite in line with some pictures of hell as a place of total, unmitigated torment. But at the same time, it is not necessarily inconsistent with many religious concepts of hell.

With this account of some of the negative aspects encountered within the NDE I will conclude my consideration of a number of recent investigations.

From the foregoing reviews of the more prominent near-death

studies that have been undertaken by contemporary American researchers, it is evident that these surveys have resulted in the accumulation of a very substantial body of descriptive data. The case history material on which these studies are based were obtained through direct personal interviews which have succeeded in demonstrating the consistency of NDEs, their recurrent features and their widespread incidence. So what is the next step? What now seems evident is that new directions in research and application related to the after-effects need to be embarked upon.

The existence and authenticity of the NDE having now been thoroughly established in America, it remains for us here in Britain to undertake a cross-cultural study in order to discover what the information obtained by a British survey can add to our understanding of the phenomenon. for it has yet to be ascertained if the same elements will be included within the near-death episodes related by British experiencers as in those reported by the American NDErs. I thus propose to show what the results of my own investigation have revealed and to compare the evidence with that of the other empirical studies of near-death phenomena that, as the foregoing narrative has shown, have been undertaken from the standpoint of several disciplines. As mentioned earlier, my own investigation has been approached from the perspective of humanistic psychology, and it is from this viewpoint that the areas of study that I intend examining are based.

The main focus of the research upon which I was engaged during the eighteen months I spent gathering information for my thesis was based on an examination of the cross-cultural aspects. During this period I conducted interviews on both sides of the Atlantic in order to ascertain if a corresponding proportion of respondents would relate similar near-death type experiences in England as those which had been reported in America, regardless of the differing cultural environments. This included noting any differences in the accounts as a result of the divergent backgrounds and also observing any relevant variance of content which could possibly have a bearing on any disparity of established NDE format.

I furthermore wanted to determine what the after-effects associated with NDEs were most likely to be and to see how the implications for transformation and self-actualisation affected the 'life-style' of the respondent. Finally, I subsequently wanted to look at the potential applications for using the knowledge gained in a psychotherapeutic or clinical setting. The objective of this work is, therefore, to show what the results of my inquiry revealed and to consider each of the questions raised and advance some theories that may possibly answer some of the issues that are still unresolved. For the implications inherent in the NDE for the development of human potential are so momentous that this aspect alone invites further investigation.

# CHAPTER 3
# *A comparative study of British near-death experiences*

Death destroys man, but the idea of death saves him.
*Forster*

Taking as my model the research methodology initiated by Kenneth Ring, I set about structuring my own inquiry according to the guidelines inaugurated by him. As my objective was to parallel a British study of the American investigation that he had undertaken, I resolved that I would follow his format as closely as was practical.

Although my research methodology was based on that employed by Dr Ring, my study of the near-death experience was based on an observation of the humanistic features involved, which included a conscious awareness of both external and internal environments. The extraordinary state of consciousness that seems to occur at the threshold of death raises the question: does a state of consciousness exist separate from the self-consciousness engendered by the brain, and are these experiences the source of many of humanity's religious doctrines and of the generally held cross-cultural belief in an afterlife? The meaning of the NDE, which obviously depends on its interpretation, is thus the major humanistic enigma to be resolved.

That the experience occurs is no longer in any doubt, for as the previous chapter has shown, systematic research with adequate documentation has now extensively endorsed the NDE. The controversy rather centres on the interpretation to be placed on the experiences: are they spurious, that is, due to some defence mechanism, whether physiological or psychological; or else are they authentic in the sense that they refer to a real spiritual state of affairs? To the near-death survivor there is seldom any uncertainty. 'There is no doubt in my mind that what I experienced was real', 'I really was there', 'It was not a dream',

'What I experienced was as real as my talking to you now', are expressions often heard. Much medical and religious opinion regards these experiences as mental deviations engendered by emotional and psychological stress due to the close proximity of death, and tends to dismiss them as being caused by hypoxic states brought on by a deteriorating nervous system in which the 'experiencer' tries to deal psychologically with anxieties about death by fantasising.

In the course of my investigation, I was able to ascertain that the NDE can occur when an individual arrives at the threshold of apparent death. During this time a state of complete interruption of bodily process occurs which is marked by an absence of all vital signs, including spontaneous function of the respiratory and circulatory system, and cessation of cerebral function, as shown by the absence of reflexes and electroencephalogram. Many of the individuals resuscitated from this state found upon recovery that they could remember having had a remarkable experience which they said occurred to them during the time that they were 'clinically dead'.

When I embarked upon my study, my hypothesis was that a significant number of respondents would relate a continuation of conscious awareness during the time that they were reported 'dead', or on the brink of 'clinical death', while not having, biologically, entirely gone. However, I realised that since a number of individuals would obviously not be in the presence of a qualified observer at the time of apparent death, it would be necessary to extend my criteria to include those respondents who had been in a life-threatening situation and who felt they had actually died. I further expected that these reports would disclose a common pattern of experiences, regardless of age, sex, religious persuasion or cultural background.

This experience, which includes a common set of elements, tends to unfold in a characteristic way that has been noted by other researchers and which has been termed the 'core experience' by Dr Ring, who proposed that there are five distinct stages of NDE. The evidence that he found during the course of his scientific investigation shows that these elements can be defined as follows. They are:

1  Peace and a sense of well-being

    2  Separation from the body
    3  Entering the darkness
    4  Seeing the light
    5  Entering the light.

The investigation of this common set of elements and the degree of cross-cultural correlation between Britain and America, associated with the approach of death, was the central challenge of my thesis.

Accepting the 'core experience' to be authentic, I was now left with the question: how common is this kind of experience in near-death episodes? According to Kübler-Ross and Moody, this kind of experience in cases of near-death survival is the rule rather than the exception, and this contention has now been largely confirmed by the recent investigation of Gallup, who by reason of the sheer scale of his operation (resulting in the mass of demographic information which his organisation was able to collect and analyse) has substantiated their claim. The reason for it not having been reported more often in the past, despite its recent prevalence due to the advances in resuscitation techniques, has been largely due to fear of ridicule and disbelief.

The chance to explore this supposition came during the summer of 1981 when I was invited by Kenneth Ring to visit him at the University of Connecticut, where the newly formed International Association for Near-Death Studies has its headquarters, in order to collaborate in the research project that he was conducting there. As my research had been following similar lines of inquiry into NDEs as those being carried out in America, we were both eager to establish cross-cultural references. The individuals chosen to be interviewed were selected from among the files of case histories in the archives of IANDS. In order to increase the frequency of positive response and to allow for collation of the material to be expedited with maximum speed, only those respondents who believed they had experienced an NDE were consulted on this occasion. I chose this method in favour of the unselected sampling procedure of the British study, as the analysis of the research material had already been undertaken and because my time for completion of the project was limited. During the course of this investigation I found ample evidence to confirm the original observations made by Kübler-Ross and Moody.

From the conversations I had with respondents in Connecticut, it became evident that they had all survived one of three distinct types of near-death onset. This included recovery from illness, accident or suicide attempt. In the group that I studied, it was evident that in some cases of illness the most complete 'core experience' was represented and included all the features of the prototype summary. Accidents furnished indications that the later stages of the 'core experience' tended to be rare, although not entirely absent. Suicide attempt was marked by an absence of the last two stages; i.e. the feeling of relief and sense of bodily detachment existed, but the experience tended to end with a feeling of confused drifting in a dark, murky void, a 'twilight zone'. Accounts strongly suggested that suicide-related near-death experiences do not reach completion but tend to fade out before the transcendent elements characteristic of the 'core experience' make their appearance.

I found that the prototype experience, despite differing circumstances and motives that brought about the near-death episode, did not generally tend to vary across the manner of near-death onset, but that the experience of dying itself, irrespective of the means that brought it about, appears to be much the same for everyone independently of how one comes close to death, and that the similarities of description, rather than the differences, are what strike one most vividly regardless of religious denomination or cultural background.

Upon my return to England, I set about notifying colleagues, friends and acquaintances of my wish to interview anyone they knew who had been resuscitated from clinical death or who felt that they had died and returned to life. I decided to use this method in the initial stages, as I wanted to see if I could reach enough people this way, thereby avoiding the drawback of having to be more specific about my research, which I felt advertising would have necessitated, thus possibly encouraging the kind of people to come forward who might be inclined to fabricate their NDE.

After I had completed my original investigation I did in fact advertise in a number of newspapers. My reason for doing this was that I wanted to see if the accounts would differ in any way as a result of using that medium. I found that in actuality there was no material difference and that the respondents who had been through an NDE obviously knew at once what my advertisement referred to and were just as sincere as those I had obtained through referral sources. Furthermore, they were, like the former respondents I had interviewed, only too pleased to be able to have an opportunity to discuss what they had experienced once they had been assured that the reason for my interest was bona fide. Like the former group I spoke to, they were also afraid to discuss their experience for fear of being ridiculed.

For my initial research, I had, as well as relying on colleagues, also used other professional contacts, including physicians, nurses, clergymen, and various staff members of a number of large hospitals, as sources of referral. My objective was to obtain access to as unbiased a sample of case history material as was feasible, so as to avoid, wherever practicable, any tendency towards 'selective' sampling procedure. This was in order to minimise, as far as possible, any likelihood of including the kind of unauthenticated testimony that has recently been appearing in the more sensational tabloids.

As a result of my visit to Connecticut, I now had a much clearer idea of how to set about structuring the proceedings. I realised that in order to get a comprehensive picture of all the aspects involved, it would be necessary to include in my study cases of NDE that had been reported as a result of having survived one of the three distinct types of near-death onset, as had been the case with the sample I had investigated in America.

My approach to the question, Which line of inquiry is it best to adopt? was influenced by the assumption that I would be able to collect my material without being unduly restricted by the considerable controversy that continues to exist over the interpretation and significance of the NDE put forward by other researchers and experiencers themselves. I felt that it was important to approach the individual reports with open-minded impartiality, as far as one is ever able to do this, since there was an obvious tendency to relate these reports as evidence of 'life after life'.

When making contact with sources of referral, I always made plain my interest in speaking to persons who had come close to death and attempted to avoid mentioning any specific concern with near-death experiences as such. Data collected from these volunteers included present age, age at the time of NDE, sex, religion, nationality and cultural background, and conditions of close encounter with death. At this point, I would like to mention that at no time was any remuneration either offered or given to those individuals who agreed to participate. Also, although none of my participants in the research project was asked to sign a consent form, they were nevertheless assured of complete confidentiality at all times.

My interview schedule involved the use of a structured consultation which was composed of four divisions of data collection information:

1  Personal information
2  A free narrative of the near-death episode
3  A series of questions designed to determine the presence or absence of the various components of the NDE
4  After-effects.

Most interviews, which were generally conducted at the home of the respondent, took about half an hour and were tape recorded whenever possible to ensure greater accuracy of transcript. Another half-hour was usually allowed for following the report, in order that questions concerning the experience and its underlying significance could be discussed, thereby avoiding any possible influence of the material by disclosures beforehand.

A factor that concerned me was that prior knowledge of near-death phenomena could significantly affect the reporting of the experience, as it became apparent at the outset of my research that not all my respondents were uninformed about NDEs. Earlier researchers had the advantage of pursuing their studies at a time when few people had any knowledge of such phenomena. By the time I undertook to cary out my own investigation, I was obliged to search out my material in the aftermath of the considerable publicity that surrounded the attention given to near-death phenomena by Elisabeth Kübler-Ross and Raymond Moody, which produced a spate of coverage in the media including a BBC television programme in the *Everyman* series, entitled *At the Hour of Death* shown in March, 1982. While the possibility existed that some respondents could have been drawn to investigate the near-death phenomenon since their near-death encounter, and that this could affect the manner in which they interpreted the basic experience (a decided disadvantage), I had nevertheless to balance this against the advantage that the greater dissemination of information had increased the willingness of people to come forward, due to the reduced threat of ridicule and disbelief arising from the more sympathetic and understanding climate that now prevails.

In assessing this factor, I routinely questioned respondents at the end of each interview about the extent, if any, of their prior or subsequent knowledge of NDEs. I was concerned to learn the source of their information, whether this was derived from direct experience alone, or whether from conversations with others about such experiences, or alternatively from near-death literature.

Another important determinant that obviously needed to be clarified in the course of any cross-cultural comparison was whether cultural and social differences would affect the noted invariance across a broad range of near-death conditions that had been observed in the Connecticut study. Cultural and social similarities and differences would clearly affect the interpretations to be placed on the experiences.

So, what appears to have emerged from my preliminary inquiry into near-death phenomena is that my study requires that I establish whether those respondents who have survived clinical death reported a significant degree of transcultural similarity, in order to conclude that the pattern of near-death experiences is probably a universal phenomenon, as the American investigation would seem to indicate.

In the following pages readers will have an opportunity to judge from the individual accounts whether this is the case. For, by citing excerpts of the phenomena encountered by respondents, I hope to illustrate some measure of the range of affective response to the experience of apparent imminent death.

# CHAPTER 4
## *Patterns of the near-death experience*

If thou wouldst complete the diamond body without
emanations,
Diligently heat the roots of consciousness and life,
Kindle Light in the blessed country ever close at hand,
And, there hidden, let thy true self eternally dwell.
*Hui Ming Ching*

During the period of about eighteen months in which I followed
up contacts and interviewed people who were reported to have
come close to death, I was able to establish what these people were
aware of having experienced, and if indeed they could recall
anything at all. The purpose of the research was to enable me to
evaluate the possibility that for a number of individuals an NDE
had apparently occurred at the time of their near-death episode.

The forty-one respondents whose case histories formed my
original study were comprised of thirty-two English and nine
American subjects and were drawn from a larger group of people
who, for one reason or another, were unable or unwilling to
participate. Although my sample was small it nevertheless
enabled me to hazard a guess as to what the evidence of this first
tentative inquiry might imply. The conclusions drawn from my
initial investigation have been reinforced since that time,
however, as I have meanwhile interviewed many more people
who claimed to have had an NDE and found that their accounts
supported my original findings, which shall be examined in the
later stages of this book.

After I had collected my material, I next took Kenneth Ring's
five stages and, using them as the basis for a comparative study,
considered each interview transcript in order to see which part of
the NDE fitted into the different categories. I found that the
respondents' testimonies clearly showed that in most cases there
was evidence of the common basic features noted by Dr Ring, and

TABLE 1
The twenty-five most generally experienced qualities encountered within
the 'core experience'

| Components of the 'core experience' | No. | % |
| --- | --- | --- |
| *Altered state of feeling* | | |
| Peace and euphoria | 18 | 47 |
| Joy and happiness | 11 | 29 |
| No more pain | 13 | 34 |
| No more fear | 6 | 16 |
| Warm and glowing | 9 | 24 |
| | | |
| *Separation from the body* | | |
| Clear view of the body | 8 | 21 |
| Suspended above the body | 12 | 32 |
| Detached and relaxed | 9 | 24 |
| Heightened awareness | 3 | 8 |
| Illuminated environment | 8 | 21 |
| | | |
| *Entering the darkness* | | |
| Dimensionless | 5 | 13 |
| Floating or drifting | 3 | 8 |
| Very rapid movement | 10 | 26 |
| Tunnel sensation | 10 | 26 |
| Rushing noise | 4 | 11 |
| | | |
| *Seeing the light* | | |
| Distant point of light | 8 | 21 |
| Magnetic pull | 2 | 5 |
| Enveloped in light and love | 15 | 39 |
| Blinding light but eyes unhurt | 6 | 16 |
| Ineffable beauty | 10 | 26 |
| | | |
| *The inner world* | | |
| Beautiful landscape and buildings | 7 | 18 |
| Heavenly music | 4 | 11 |
| Brilliant glowing colours | 7 | 18 |
| Feeling of oneness | 8 | 21 |
| Telepathic communication | 10 | 26 |

Of the forty-one people interviewed, thirty-eight described an event that
fell within the category of the 'core experience' and these are the ones
represented in this analysis.

that the consistent pattern of the 'core experience' is, moreover, inclined to be revealed in a particular sequence regardless of nationality. Not all the successive phases were perceived by everyone, and not everyone who had experienced a close encounter with death necessarily had an NDE. Furthermore, the earlier stages of the experience are the most frequent, while the later stages are presented less and less frequently, as it appears that the 'deeper' the stage experienced, the fewer the people who revive to report the experience.

When interviewing my sample of respondents I attempted to keep to Dr Ring's pattern wherever possible, bearing in mind that this was to be a comparative study, and in general I think the model I adopted basically resembles the one used by Dr Ring (1980).

I will from this point on be drawing upon numerous examples of case histories taken from the respondents themselves, in order to illustrate the numinous quality that these narratives convey; for, by allowing the experience to speak directly to the reader, I hope to transmit something of the essence of what appears to take place at the moment of the NDE. Therefore, having delineated the five distinct categories of the 'core experience', I now propose to describe these five phases by reference to specific interviews.

## FIRST PHASE: PEACE AND A SENSE OF WELL-BEING

The first phase relates to the conscious experience of dying, which is heralded by a feeling of such peace and well-being that most respondents say that there are no words to describe it. However, in attempting to do so the narrative is often so deeply moving and compelling that the impression which they convey is frequently more profound than words.

A number of typical examples of the kind of statement made in regard to this experience are quoted in the following excerpts.

A woman who nearly died from the very protracted birth of her daughter said: 'the peace and happiness that I felt are impossible to describe.' And an American woman who suffered a heart attack recalled: 'What I can never forget is the absolute feeling of peace and joy.' As can readily be seen from these statemens given by two women from different continents, the similarity of description is most striking. In the excerpts that follow, the reader will have an opportunity to discern many such examples of the almost identical accounts of both English and American NDErs.

An Englishman who was clinically 'dead' for two hours as a result of pneumonia and pleurisy stated: 'It was a wonderful feeling. In the peace, beauty, joy and, above all, love, I felt more truly alive than I ever have before.' An American who almost died as the result of a haemorrhage following an operation for the removal of haemorrhoids described his experience in a similar way: 'It is beyond description. I was one with pure light and love. I was one with God and at the same time one with everything.' Another woman who felt she 'died' from a virus infection of the spinal cord found: 'I then passed into another dimension. I felt no pain anymore and was conscious of the most wonderful golden light. A feeling of absolute peace and bliss flooded over me.'

Although there are many more passages that could be included to illustrate this phase of the 'core experience', I feel that the ones I have given serve to convey the power of feeling that these people express when attempting to communicate what they feel when confronted with the onset of apparent death. So I will conclude this section with one final excerpt.

A woman who felt she had died following two major operations in two days said of her experience:

> All pain disappeared, comfort seized me. Only my essence was felt. Time no longer mattered and space was filled with bliss. I was bathed in radiant light and immersed in the aura of the rainbow. All was fusion. Sounds were of a new order, harmonious, nameless (now I call it music).

The analysis of feeling, taken from the case histories of both English and American near-death experiencers, revealed that more than half reported an extremely positive sensation, though not all to the same extent. The non-experiencers, on the other hand, were for the most part not conscious of having had any emotions during their near-death episode. Interestingly enough, only a small proportion of the respondents recounted an experience that was characterised by predominantly unpleasant feelings or imagery. The few near-death episodes that did include alarming and negative aspects, I will deal with in a separate category. In the meantime I will continue with the descriptions of the successive phases of the 'core experience'.


## SECOND PHASE: SEPARATION FROM THE BODY

The second phase of the 'core experience' involves a sense of leaving the body behind. Admittedly, although some people reported that though they had a feeling of bodily separation they could not actually see themselves, over 50 per cent of the respondents claimed to have had visually clear out-of-the-body experiences.

Accounts of this phase of the experience naturally varied with individuals, but typically they tended to find themselves in the room above the body, often in a corner, looking down at their prostrate form as if they were a spectator. They usually state that at the time this seemed quite natural, and also report a heightened but detached mental process, more acute hearing, and a very brightly illuminated environment. This situation is described as being distinctly real. They feel as much alive as before, in fact many of the respondents reported feeling more alive and were conscious of everything that was happening. During this period the individual can be observed to have reached the stage of brain death, with complete cessation of neurological function, deep unconsciousness without response to painful stimuli and without any EEG electrical activity. The following accounts are typical of this phase of the experience.

A woman recalled her heart attack as follows:

> I was in the intensive care unit of Worthing hospital. During the early hours, I found myself suspended above my body looking down at myself. I heard and saw two doctors and a nurse running towards the bed and heard them say 'quick, quick'. I am sure I had died.

And a woman who had nearly died as a result of complications which developed after a tonsillectomy observed: I remember that absolutely beautiful feeling of peace and happiness. I was above, I don't know where, but I was definitely up. I didn't have a body, but at the same time it was definitely up there. A woman who was suffering from hyperventilation recalled:

> I was with a neighbour arranging to have my children looked after as I was feeling so unwell and I wanted my husband to take me to my doctor. Suddenly for no reason I got a severe pain and muscle spasm down the left side of my body, with a burning sensation. I called out to my friend and as she came into the room I collapsed onto the floor. Then everything went black. I opened my eyes but everything was still black. I could hear quite clearly and knew I was not unconscious. Then suddenly I realised I was standing up by the door and could see my body lying on the floor. I could see everything that was going on. I was convinced that I was dying as my heart felt as if it had stopped beating, whereas before it had been pounding. Also the pain had ceased.

Another woman who was haemorrhaging following an operation for the removal of fibroids in her womb related:

> I remember coming round from the anaesthetic and then drifting off and finding myself out of my body, over the bed looking down at my carcass. I was aware only of being a brain and eyes, I do not remember having a body. The next thing I realised was that I was neither a woman nor a man, just pure spirit. I could see the doctors and nurses round my bed frantically trying to give me a blood transfusion. They were having difficulty finding a vein in my arm. I was amused at all this fuss going on with my body as it did not concern me a bit.

Although this woman could see her body quite clearly, she was nevertheless not aware of being in another body as such, but rather, she was conscious only of being an entity. This sense of being in some sort of formless dimension was reported by most of the respondents during this phase, but while they did not seem to have any recognisable form, they were still conscious of being themselves.

A man who had been in hospital undergoing treatment for leukaemia also referred to this sense of spiritual identity:

> I became aware of my spirit, or whatever you want to call it, being up in a corner of the room and looking down on my body with doctors and nurses, and all the people and hospital paraphernalia being brought into the room and piled on my chest and so forth. I could not feel any of this at the time it was happening, but I was like a spectator looking down on this from up in the corner of the room. I didn't have any regrets or anything, it just felt kind of strange.

Whether aware of being in a body or not, whether suspended above their body or viewing it from a standing position, what all these respondents stress is that, while they are convinced that they were either 'dead' or dying, they were nevertheless equally certain that their conscious memory and sense of personal identity survived.

Another aspect of this phase of the 'core experience' that occurs frequently enough to warrant a special mention is the feature of illumination.

A woman whose specific conditions were never satisfactorily diagnosed, but whose physician regarded her near-death episode as likely evidence of a heart attack, remembered:

> I experienced a very severe pain. I felt I was going to die. The pain spread through every part of my body, even my fingers and toes. It was so bad I was unable to speak. I could see my face in the mirror which was ashen. I then passed into another dimension.

A man who nearly died following an operation for a double strangulated hernia recalled:

> I was suddenly conscious of all around me, although I couldn't move or speak. Then I was aware of looking down on my bed and seeing myself, a shrivelled old man, a pitiful lifeless being. I was next aware of indescribably beautiful colours and a brightness most intense.

A second hyperventilation case who had been treated in the cardiac ward of Charing Cross Hospital observed: 'I suddenly became aware I was floating above myself and all the fear and panic seemed to go. I was calm and everything was very bright. I felt peaceful and warm. It was really beautiful.' And a woman who was in intensive care for twelve days following a serious car accident said: 'During this time I was surrounded by lovely soft glowing colours.'

Also worthy of note are the visual and auditory perceptions reported by respondents while allegedly out of the body. The excerpts already quoted touch on this subject; other examples are more striking in that the experiencers appeared to have been able to observe objects that they would not normally have been able to see from the position that the body was in.

A woman whose near-death event had resulted from a prolonged and difficult labour during childbirth gave the following account:

> As the pain reached its peak it suddenly stopped and I found myself suspended up under the ceiling. I could not see myself, there was some mist below and as I leaned over to try to see under my body I had the sensation that I would fall down. Although I couldn't see my body I could nevertheless see everything in the room, like the telephone which was not visible from the bed, I could see quite clearly from my position above. I could also hear everything that was going on and the nurse who was still trying to get me to move my leg. Then I heard her say, 'My God, she's gone.'

A man related the ensuing experience following a cardiac arrest:

> They took me into the emergency room and I guess they started working on me at this point. I guess at this point I left my body as I seemed to be up above the room. I had never been in this room before, I was unconscious when they brought me in. I was above the room in a corner and I could see the doctors, as clear as a bell, working on me. . . . One said, 'I think he's gone, let's try some electrical thing'; I don't know what it was. They put a pad on me and then they put these electrical things on me and said something about mega volts. They must have started up my heart or something of that sort, I knew nothing more until I opened my eyes and I was in the intensive care unit. Now I looked up and there's these guys I've never seen before and they were the same people I had seen while I was unconscious. About a month later I wanted to make sure this was not a hallucination or

something of that sort and I went back to this hospital and I asked the nurse to show me this room which I had never seen in my life before and I walked in there and I knew where everything was. It was all there, the table, the lights, the cabinet, everything, like I remembered.

A man who was clinically dead for two hours as a result of pneumonia and pleurisy recounted his experience in the following way:

I was in Crumpsall Hospital near Manchester . . . I can still picture the scene. I saw myself lying on the bed. I saw a young nurse. She was preparing me for the mortuary. I remember thinking at the time how young she was to have to do such a thing as getting me ready and even shaving me. I actually saw it taking place. I was detached from it, it was as if I was there watching and I was the third party. I felt no emotion, just nothing, like looking at a picture. I was clinically dead about two hours . . . and I woke up at the mortuary of Crumpsall Hospital and it was the mortuary attendant who nearly had a heart attack! I know it wasn't a dream.

As well as the dramatic aspect of visual and auditory perceptions, another feature that was commented on by a number of respondents was a voice which commanded them to go back and return to their body.

A student who was nearly asphyxiated during a bout of croup remembered having this experience:

I was very ill and had great difficulty breathing. One evening I woke about nine o'clock from sleep realising something was prompting me to wake up and I realised I could not breathe. My eyes were popping out of my head and I was aware I was being asphyxiated. I can remember trying to rouse my sister who was asleep in the same room with me, but as I couldn't breathe this wasn't possible. I told myself to relax and accept that I was unable to breathe and just lay there waiting to die. By this time I was unable to close my eyes. Then I realised that I was starting to move upwards towards the ceiling and I thought I was going to bang myself on the ceiling at any minute and turned to avoid hitting the ceiling and as I did so I saw myself lying on the bed and I thought I looked very ill, terrible with great bags under my eyes. I felt weightless and I somehow moved through the ceiling which was no longer important. I was aware of going faster and faster. I wasn't frightened, but I wondered where I was going. Suddenly I heard a stern male voice above me which said, 'Get back, get back in there.' With that I found myself back in bed in a split second. I have no idea how I got there but I gasped for breath and sat up coughing blood. I managed to rouse my sister and told her what had happened but she said it was obviously because I was feverish. But I know the experience was totally real.

The woman who was in Charing Cross Hospital after an attack of hyperventilation stated: 'Next I heard a voice, which I am sure was my mother's, saying, "No, you must go back." ' From a woman who endured prolonged labour giving birth:

At this point I heard a man's voice, it was not anyone I recognised, saying, 'You must go back.' It was a kind voice but very firm and he was saying, 'Remember the baby, who's going to look after it? You must go back.'

And from a woman who was taken unconscious to hospital suffering from a fractured skull after being knocked down by a car:

Then I heard a voice, it was not an English voice, but it sounded foreign, saying, 'Margaret, go back, go back.' I next felt as if a blind was pulled down and I shot back into my conscious state and woke up in the hospital bed.

Finally, I will end my account of this phase of the 'core experience' with a description of the near-death episode of a psychotherapist living in London. His experience includes a very interesting aspect concerning the suspension of time during out-of-the-body states. While undergoing his heart attack he observed:

I was working at home with a student whom I was supervising. After about ten minutes I began to get a pain down my left arm. I tried to ignore it but it got worse very quickly and after about ten minutes I had to stop the session.

> I then got a very severe pain in my chest which doubled me
> up. I managed to reach the phone in the hall and rang the
> ambulance service. By this time the pain had become very,
> very bad and I was soaked to the skin with sweat. I curled up
> on the floor waiting for the ambulance team to arrive. Then
> suddenly it [the pain] stopped and I wondered when the
> ambulance would arrive. I looked at my watch to see how
> long it would take them and I realised my watch had
> stopped, which was most unusual as it was an electronic
> tuning fork watch in very good condition. This may sound
> strange but I felt I needed some timing device, so I felt for my
> pulse and there was none. I got quite frightened and was also
> puzzled as well. I then put my hand on my chest and could
> feel no heartbeat. There was a strange shift in perception at
> this time and I realised I was above the stairs looking down
> the stairs and I actually considered throwing myself down
> the stairs, in order to start my heart beating again. I could
> not see my body from the stairs nor was I aware of being out
> of my body at the time.

After the ambulance team arrived and he had been resuscitated, he
discovered his watch had restarted at the exact time he had
're-entered' his body. He knew this as it was slow by precisely the
period of time that he was apparently 'dead'.

However one chooses to interpret this phase of the phenomenon, I have found that physicians, in attempting to explain
the NDE, traditionally start with the assumption that visual and
auditory perceptions are always a direct and indivisible function
of the physical organism and can under no circumstances occur
outside the confines of brain and body. Advocates of this
approach have concluded that out-of-the-body experiences,
near-death or otherwise, are simply not possible regardless of how
'real' they seemed to be at the time. Explanations of the apparent
contradictions are therefore sought in order to find some physical
or psychological mechanism to account for the phenomenon. But
to date it seems that no adequate explanations have been found.

Having duly reviewed the accounts that contained descriptions
of resuscitation events and, wherever possible, sought to confirm
the information with members of the medical team, or
alternatively to obtain testimonies from others who were present

at the time of the near-death event, I am obliged to conclude from the evidence I found that somehow it would seem that conscious awareness survives physical death.


## THIRD PHASE: ENTERING THE DARKNESS

In the third phase of the 'core experience' people go through a dark transitional period which appears to be a passage between one state of being and another, leading on to other realms of perception. This journey forward has been described as feeling that one is in a vast black space, through which one is moving at great speed. A number of respondents experienced this phenomenon as travelling through a dark tunnel. The following excerpts will illustrate the characteristics of this phase of the experience.

A woman who was in a coma due to kidney infection resulting from an allergic reaction to penicillin gave this account:

> It was as if I was waking up from being asleep and yet I was not dreaming. I found myself walking down a tunnel which seemed to widen out. I remember the most wonderful feeling of peace. When you try to recapture the feeling, however happy you are, it is just not the same.

A man who had been in hospital having an arteriogram for a cyst on his kidney recollected: 'I suddenly found myself travelling through a dark tunnel at a terrific speed. I was completely weightless. I can remember the experience as clearly as if it happened yesterday.' Another man whose heart and respiration failed three times as a result of pneumonia arising out of a gall bladder operation found: 'At some point I started to feel very comfortable. The pain and fear left me and I found myself travelling down a very black tube.'

While the foregoing passages reveal that a number of respondents found themselves entering the darkness as though they were travelling through a tunnel, some people also described the experience in terms of being in outer space.

A respondent who was in hospital to have an emergency operation for heart disease put her experiences this way: 'I remember being taken into the operating theatre. The next thing I remember is feeling as if I was rushing through space at a great speed.' Another woman remembered: 'As I lost consciousness I can remember feeling as if I was rushing through black space at a tremendous speed.' While a woman who evidently nearly died while under the anaesthetic for a tooth extraction recalled:

> During this time I found myself out of my body, standing beside the dentist, and I remember feeling frightened looking down at my body and thinking I must be dead. Then everything went black and I felt myself rushing through the blackness at such speed that it's impossible to compare it to anything.

One man put his account of this phase the following way: 'I then passed right through the ceiling and the wall, right out into the blackness. I was still in a horizontal position and I seemed to be passing through a real black area; there were no lights or anything.'

Although a few people recalled either going through a tunnel or alternatively found themselves in black space, for a number of NDErs, however, this period was characterised by a sensation that they were not only in space but that this vastness somehow assumed the dimensions of a tunnel which drew them towards an opening as the speed increased.

A woman who felt she had 'died' stated: 'I found myself in a black space and I knew that I was no longer in my body. I was aware of whirling round and round at great speed. It felt as if I was in a tunnel.' Another woman said in regard to this phase:

> I was in what felt like outer space. It was absolutely black out there and I felt like I was being drawn towards an opening like at the end of a tunnel. I knew this because I could see a light at the end; that's how I knew it was there. I was vertical and I was being drawn towards the opening. I know it wasn't a dream, dreams just don't happen that way. I never once imagined it was a dream.

To end this phase of the 'core experience' I will include a final account which gives a very detailed description. It comes from an American accident victim who 'died' when he was crushed under a truck:

I passed out for the third time. By now the pain and the pressure were gone and I wasn't really sure what was going on. I could see O.K. and I felt pretty good, but nothing made any sense. I tried looking around as I just wasn't sure where I really was. Then everything went dark. It was like waking up in outer space or in total darkness. I had no sensation of hot or cold; I can't really explain what it felt like, but it's just a huge vastness of just nothing. The next thing I realised was a feeling of motion. I was moving forward and I had the sensation that the speed was increasing. As I went faster and faster the void gradually assumed the shape of a tunnel, like the inside of a tornado. The dimension of the tunnel could be thousands of miles wide. As you go further forward into the tunnel you have the feeling of going into infinity. You have a feeling of free falling but you are not falling down, more a sensation of moving forward or going through. By now I felt as if I was being propelled forward at the speed of light or faster, in a straight line.

From my limited data it appears at this time that the tunnel experience is inclined to be encountered slightly more frequently by American NDErs, while the accounts of British NDErs would seem to suggest that they are more likely to move straight from the out-of-the-body stage to the fourth or fifth phase of the 'core experience'. Of course, this may well depend on the category that one selects for a particular experience, for the phases often contain elements of each other which make for a merging of the aspects, so that there is frequently no clear dividing line. Whether this will eventually prove to be otherwise when I have collected more reports, only time will tell. Meanwhile it appears that however the experience is described, whether moving rapidly through a dark tunnel or simply finding oneself in a vast black void, what is undoubtedly being experienced during this phase is a very unusual state of consciousness.

This is the point where, from now on, an extraordinary transcendent quality is evident, leading to the state where those people who have encountered this phenomenon feel certain that what they glimpsed during their NDE may well have been a preview of what lies beyond the frontiers of death.

## FOURTH PHASE: SEEING THE LIGHT

The move to the fourth phase of the 'core experience' from the preceding one is marked by the notable appearance of the light which heralds the beginning of an entirely new dimension of the experience. This light is usually seen as a very brilliant white or golden light, but can on occasions also be discerned as blue. This light, which is described as being so bright that it would normally be blinding, does not however hurt the eyes. Everything appears to be suffused in its radiance and the colours are notable for their vividness and intensity. Many people report feeling enveloped by this light and state that it is warm and uplifting and of ineffable beauty. Some respondents said that they felt it was a living light. At all events, this move from darkness into the light is seen by many as heralding the dawn of a new state of existence.

Sometimes the light is first encountered when drawing near to the end of the tunnel, as was the case with a man who had been given last rites during his near-death crisis:

> I found myself travelling towards a light which was very drawing. I don't remember thinking that this light was anything unusual, just that it was light at the other end of the tunnel and I was conscious of being lifted up. Finally I seemed to arrive at this very lighted area; it was just total comfort and ease.

While one of the women who nearly died in childbirth experienced moving into the light which she encountered at the end of the tunnel:

> I was moving very rapidly down a long dark tunnel. I seemed to be floating. I saw faces which came and went and who looked at me kindly, but did not communicate. I did not recognise them. As I got nearer to the end of the tunnel I seemed to be surrounded by a wonderful warm glowing light.

And a woman who had cardiac disease gave this description:

> The next thing I remember was being carried or projected very rapidly through what appeared to be a cylindrical void.

I could see in the distance a light, very bright light. As I rapidly came closer to this light it grew brighter and wider. I heard sounds around me that appeared or felt almost like an echo, but they were not frightening; they were vibrations . . . more than anything else. As I came closer to this light it grew so bright and so all encompassing, I found myself suddenly totally surrounded and submerged in this beautiful light.

Whereas the man who was suffering from leukaemia experienced the light this way:

Like the sun coming up in a valley between two mountains. I knew that there were people down there in the valley, but I could not see them. I kept looking because I knew there were people down there. Then after a while I became aware that this light that I had seen in the distance was drawing nearer and nearer. I was coming up on it and I could see a figure standing in the light, like in the V of the mountain. At that time I didn't pay much attention as I was still looking for those people down below me. Suddenly, I seemed to be right in front of the being standing there. He was standing with the light behind him and I had the dark behind me so I was actually facing the light.

Two of these respondents were aware of other beings who were also in the blackness with them at the time they passed through, although they could not make out who they were or what they were doing there. Furthermore, a being of light was mentioned by several NDErs in relation to this phase of the 'core experience' and also during the next.

Another man who nearly died as a result of a ruptured ulcer in the small intestine said of his near-death event:

The experience I had at this time was total beauty. To go through the pain and all up to that point, well I don't think I could go through it again, but at the end it was so beautiful that I am not afraid of it. It was total peacefulness. The light was extremely bright but it wasn't a harsh light. I don't know if I was conscious of the lights in the operating room or whether it was a vision, I have no way of knowing one way or the other. I have no recollection of any events leading up to this experience, I just found myself in this extremely bright light and felt absolute peace. I feel the light and the peace were one. All I know is that I was there, I'm not afraid of it and that it's something beautiful. I just can't explain it. I don't remember how I got there, just that I was suddenly in the light and it was beautiful. I had no sense of separate identity. I was in the light and one with it.

Also from another woman whose near-death experience resulted from a hysterectomy:

I became aware at some point that I was having a very unusual experience. I found myself in a place full of radiant light. It's quite unlike anything you could possibly imagine on this earth. The light is brighter than anything you could possibly imagine. There are no words to describe it. I was so happy, it's impossible to explain. It was such a feeling of serenity, it was a marvellous feeling. The light is so bright that it would normally blind you, but it doesn't hurt one's eyes a bit.

On other occasions the light can be experienced in the context of the tunnel itself, as was the case with one of the respondents who was told by her doctor, after coming out of her operation to have her womb removed, that she was a 'borderline case', meaning that she was near death. She recalled the incident in the following way:

I was in a long shining tunnel. It was dark behind me and I could see light at the other end. All around me the walls of the tunnel were all shining. I seemed to be floating along, but I couldn't go forward as I wanted to see my children and husband again.

Occasionally the light is perceived as blue, as is evidenced by the following accounts. An accident victim recalled:

During the night I started to feel as if I was falling down and down a well, which was going round and round. At the end of this deep well I could see a wonderful blue light which was coming up and enveloping me. It was alive, like a living light. I could hear beautiful music all around me. I felt as if I was going back somewhere I belonged. There were people all around who I sensed were loving friends.

A man who nearly died of pneumonia recounted:

A blue-gold light which appeared and grew brighter and brighter. I went forward towards the light and as I did so I had such a feeling of freedom and joy, it's beyond words to explain. I had a boundless sense of expansion.

While another man narrated his experience thus:

Then gradually you realise that way, way off in the distance, an unmeasurable distance, you may be reaching the end of the tunnel, as you can see a white light, but it's so far away I can only compare it to looking up into the sky and in the distance seeing a single star, but visually you must remember that you are looking through a tunnel and this light would fill the end of the tunnel. You concentrate on this speck of light because as you are propelled forward you anticipate reaching this light. Gradually as you travel towards it at an extreme speed it gets larger and larger. The whole process on reflection only seems to take about one minute. As you gradually draw nearer to this extremely brilliant light there is no sensation of an abrupt end of the tunnel, but rather more of a merging into the light. By now the tunnel is behind you and before you is this magnificent, beautiful blue-white light. The brilliance is so bright, brighter than a light that would immediately blind you, but absolutely does not hurt your eyes at all.

One young man who was on the point of committing suicide by taking an overdose of mandrax tablets had this experience: 'Suddenly without warning a bolt of light enveloped me and I was overpowered by feelings of such peace that there are no words to describe it.'

In the following two instances one English, one American, a sense of vibration or radiation is experienced. Whereas in the case quoted of the woman with heart disease who was aware of sounds which (as near as she could get to describing them) were more like vibrations, here we have two cases of vibrations being expressed as felt, rather than heard. The first was experienced by the psychotherapist who suffered a nearly fatal heart attack. During the ensuing crisis, what happened was as follows:

> I then felt my body begin to tingle, followed by the sensation that every cell in my body was vibrating. As this increased my whole body glowed. It was very beautiful and incredibly comforting. It wasn't as if I was taken somewhere, but it was as if I allowed this to continue there would be no coming back. But it isn't death, that's not the right word.

The second experience was undergone by one of the heart attack victims in Connecticut. He related the event in this way:

> After this the most beautiful golden light, it was like an archway there and this beautiful feeling of warmth came into my body and I started to radiate. I came into the arc of pure golden love and light. This radiation of love entered me and instantly I was part of it and it was part of me.

Although most of the core experiencers reported a sense of being completely detached from their bodies, whether they claimed to be able to see themselves or not, they were nevertheless mostly aware of being in a form which they were clearly conscious of and which, as we will see during the next phase, was clearly recognisable to others, but which was somehow more etheric and less solid than the body they had just 'vacated'.

Whatever the explanation may be for this phase of the near-death incident, many respondents felt that the light was somehow symbolic, that it was the precursor of glad tidings, a 'messenger of joy', proclaiming an end to the time of darkness and offering promise of the dawn of new life. From this point on, the light no longer served as a guide nor enveloped the experiencer in a warm and glowing radiance. It now illuminated the 'world within', as perceived through the gates of death, and was understood to be the source from which all life and love springs.


## FIFTH PHASE: THE INNER WORLD

This is the phase where people report that they feel themselves entering a 'world' in which the light appears to have its origin. This 'world within' is one of surpassing beauty. The colours are described as being 'out of this world', in fact many of the descriptions do not seem to correspond exactly to anything in this world. At this stage, respondents claim to find deceased loved ones waiting to greet them. They may report seeing wonderful landscapes and buildings, or claim to have seen beautiful flowers and trees. A number asserted that they had heard preternatural harmonies, regarded as the 'music of the spheres'. I found that only about one-third of the respondents gave evidence of penetrating to this final phase. A number of those who did expressed resentment at this point for reluctantly being brought back to life. For after having experienced a love and a beauty that surpasses anything known on this earth, they were understandably disinclined to return to a world of ordinary reality. What follows are the accounts of those individuals who, prior to being snatched back from imminent death, felt almost without exception that they were afforded a glimpse of what they generally regarded to be the 'afterlife'.

A typical example of this phase of the 'core experience' was given by a woman who was in intensive care after she suffered a heart attack:

> I don't know how I got there, but I found myself in a beautiful country lane. I was strolling down the lane slowly and I felt I had all the time in the world. I could hear the sky larks singing and I thought 'Oh, how lovely.' I particularly noticed the colours; the sky was a brilliant blue, but the colours were so soft. The green of the trees, too, was brilliant but not harsh. I felt myself bathed in a beautiful warmth and was aware of the sunlight which was brilliant but not harsh. I could not see the sun, but was aware of the light and warmth. I looked down the lane and could see a long way into the distance. Time didn't seem to matter, I felt I had all the time in the world just to stroll down the lane and enjoy the feeling of peace and serenity. I felt light and buoyant. I felt something was waiting for me at the end of the lane, but I felt there was no need to hurry as I had all the time in the world. I was aware that had I continued down the lane and reached the end, I would not have returned.

A similar description came from a woman who was very badly burnt when the back of the crinoline dress she was wearing for a

New Year's Eve fancy dress party caught alight. She was rushed to hospital but her burns were so severe that she was not expected to last through the night:

> At some point I suddenly found myself in this beautiful place. I was greeted by such warmth and happiness that it was utter bliss. I was in a beautiful landscape, the flowers, trees, the colours were indescribable, not at all like the colours you see here. The peace and joy were overpowering. I felt warm and glowing. There was a blinding light, but it was not harsh and did not hurt my eyes. The beauty of the landscape is beyond description. Somewhere I heard the most wonderful music and there was an organ playing as well. I felt embraced by such love, it's beyond description.

And a woman whose heart stopped while she was under the anaesthetic during a dental extraction told me:

> Then I found myself, I was in a beautiful landscape, the grass is greener than anything seen on earth, it has a special light or glow. The colours are beyond description, the colours here are so drab by comparison. The light is brighter than anything possible to imagine. There are no words to describe it, it's a heavenly light. In this place I saw people that I knew had died. There were no words spoken, but it was as if I knew what they were thinking and at the same time I knew that they knew what I was thinking. I felt a peace that passed all understanding. It was a marvellous feeling. I felt exhilarated and felt I was one with everything. I saw Christ but the light coming from Him was so bright that it would normally blind you. I felt as if I wanted to stay there for ever, but someone, I felt it was my guardian angel, said, 'You have to go back as you have not finished your term.' Then I felt a kind of vibrating and I was back again.

This sense of 'other-worldliness' was also brought out in the account of a woman suffering from heart disease who was discovered at her home in a coma three days after her heart attack. When she was taken to hospital she had a cardiac arrest before eventually recovering:

> I seemed to find myself in what appeared to be some type of

structure or building, but there were no walls that I can remember. There was only this all-pervading beautiful golden light. I felt extremely peaceful. I felt totally lacking in any fear, any concern. I felt very much that I belonged where I was at that moment. I noticed about me many people that seemed to be walking or milling about; they didn't even appear to walk, but seemed somehow to glide. I didn't feel apart from them at all; one of the feelings I remember most about them was the feeling of unity, of being totally a part of everything around me and about me. There was no separateness at all. The peace that I felt was indescribable, it was something I have never known before and I have never been able to reach again, even in moments of meditation or great beauty. I saw my parents approaching me, they appeared as I always remembered them to be. They seemed not at all surprised to see me, in fact they looked as if they were waiting for me and saying, 'We've been waiting for you.' I know we communicated some things and I believe many things, but I don't remember really what they were. I know that I was in the surroundings of something very beautiful, very spiritual. I can only say that I believe that I was in a state of total cosmic consciousness. I know that I communicated with my parents and with people around me, but it was not in words, it was a form of telepathic communication. I seemed to be told or made aware of telepathically that I would be seeing or talking to possibly someone that I believed to be God or Christ, I don't know. I felt tremendous peace and oneness, the unity was indescribable. The surroundings were or appeared to be marble, in structure pillars. There seemed to be something in front of me that looked like a crypt or something that I had to walk up to. There were stairs and it was also marble or it appeared to be. Also, possibly a long table and I felt that I would be communicating or talking with someone there. But suddenly I was communicated to by someone, possibly my father, that I must come back, that I could not stay, that it was not time for me, that there was much that I had to do and that I had to return.

The passage just quoted was taken from the transcript of an American woman whose case was included in my sample and who, in Kenneth Ring's opinion, had the deepest experience of any respondent he encountered during the Connecticut study. He points out in *Life at Death* that 'she not only had a glimpse of the world that appears to individuals in stage V, but in addition, received some quite detailed visual impressions'. In the following account, which comes from a man whose death certificate had been signed and whose burial preparations were in the process of being arranged while he was purported to be dead, a very deep level of experience was also reached. His narrative continued:

I arrived at a place – it's very hard to put this into words, but I can only describe it as heaven. It's a place of intense light, a place of intense activity, more like a bustling city than a lonely country scene, nothing like floating on clouds or harps or anything of that sort. While I was there I felt at the centre of things. I felt enlightened and cleansed. I felt I could see the point of everything. Everything fitted in, it all made sense, even the dark times. It almost seemed, too, as if the pieces of a jig-saw all fitted together. You know how it is with tapestry, how you see the back of the tapestry and all the interwoven parts, then when the tapestry's turned over you see how it all fits into place. Suddenly I saw how all my life fitted together to that point. I could have been there for ever and ever. I saw Jesus Christ. I was aware of him by the print of nails in his hands and his feet and I remember I was very amused. I thought it was a joke at the time, it made me laugh, and other people laughed with me; I think there must be humour in heaven. I said, 'You know, these are the only man-made things in heaven.' I thought it was wildly funny. I don't know why, but it just appealed to me at the time particularly. Because of my relationship to him and the way he looked at me, I knew that there was no need to worry or to be afraid. There was no sense of time. In a way it seemed as though everyone dies at the same time and so heaven is a great reunion experience. Our normal spatio-temporal vocabulary is frustratingly inadequate to describe heaven. The people I recognised whilst dead were my mother and grandmother, and although I could not have recognised them, I was aware of such giants as Peter and Paul and the founder of the Church Army, Wilson Carlisle. There were also numerous Christian people I have known in life. I especially recognised the Sunday School teacher called Frank, who influenced me a great deal and who lost his life in the Second World War. I think that I was surrounded by what I can only describe as a reception committee. Frank was one of these. Another was my saintly Roman Catholic doctor who had just previously died. These are the people who enjoyed my 'joke'. They did have a physical shape; it's hard to describe, but it somehow combined the youth and vigour of twenty-one-year-olds, with a sense of perfect maturity. As for Jesus, in that place of light, Jesus was the light itself. This does not mean he was an abstraction, he was as much a 'person' as all the others. He was prophet, priest and king. I knew him by the nail holes in his hands and feet, and by the way he looked at me. I shall never forget the look of Jesus. It was a searching look which saw every part of me, but I realised that he could not take his eyes off me because he loved me so much. Love is the major impression I still retain. In heaven there is light, peace, music, beauty and joyful activity, but above all there is love and within this love I felt more truly alive than I have ever done before.

Another man who reached the fifth phase recounted his experience of entering the light this way:

The following series of events appear to happen simultaneously but in describing them I will have to take them one at a time. The sensation is of a being of some kind, more a kind of energy, not a character in the sense of another person, but an intelligence with whom it is possible to communicate. Also, in size it just covers the entire vista before you. It totally engulfs everything, you feel enveloped. The light immediately communicates to you, in an instant telekinesis your thought waves are read, regardless of language. A doubtful statement would be impossible to receive. The first message I received was 'relax, everything is beautiful, everything is O.K. you have nothing to fear'. I was immediately put at absolute ease. In the past if someone like a doctor had said 'it's O.K. you have nothing to fear, this won't hurt,' it usually did – you couldn't trust them. But this was the most beautiful feeling I have ever known, it's

absolute pure love. Every feeling, every emotion is just
perfect. You feel warm, but it has nothing to do with
temperature. Everything there is absolutely vivid and clear.
What the light communicates to you is a feeling of true, pure
love. You experience this for the first time ever. You can't
compare it to the love of your wife, or the love of your
children or sexual love. Even if all those things were
combined, you cannot compare it to the feeling you get from
this light.

The next account, which comes from an elderly lady who
suffered a heart attack, includes a very provocative aspect of the
phenomenon, which concerns paranormal knowledge of future
events. This feature, while infrequent, is one that has nevertheless
also been noted by other researchers and is consistent with the
assertion that on occasions near-death experiences have been
known to disclose precognitive information:

I found myself standing in front of a nice prefab [inexpensive
and prefabricated dwelling that can be erected very quickly
and was extensively used during World War Two to house
bombed-out victims]. There was a path leading up to the
front door with masses of nasturtiums on either side. The
door was open and I could see my mother inside. I thought,
'That's funny, my mum always wanted a prefab and she
always loved nasturtiums.' I went up to the door and said,
'I've brought you a present, mum.' It was some lovely blue
silk, enough to make a dress. She took the material and put it
on the table and then got out a pair of scissors. I said, 'Mum,
what are you doing? You know you don't know how to do
dress-making.' She said, 'It's all right, they've been teaching
me since I got here.' I could see my Uncle Alf inside; I never
cared for him much in this life. They seemed to be getting
ready for a visitor, as if they were expecting someone. I said,
'Can I come in?' It looked so nice and welcoming, but my
mother said, 'No, you can't, it's not your time to stay.' I said,
'Please, mum, it's so lovely here, I don't want to go back.'
But she was very firm and would not allow me to cross the
threshold. I said, 'You seem to be expecting someone; if it's
not me, then who are you expecting?' She said, 'We are
getting ready for your Auntie Ethel. She is expected shortly.'

I begged once again if she would let me come in, as it was so warm and sunny and I felt really happy and at peace there. I did not want to go back, but she would not allow me to come in. The next thing I remember is finding myself back in bed at the hospital. I had been unconscious for three days. The nurse said to me, 'You gave us a real scare, we all thought you were a goner.' A day or two later my family were allowed in to see me and they all looked very glum. I said, 'I don't know what you are all looking so glum for, I haven't died yet, you won't get rid of me so easily.' They said they had some bad news and didn't know if they should tell me as I had been so ill, nearly dying and all. So I said, 'You might as well tell me now that you've said that much.' And they said that since I had been in hospital my Auntie Ethel had unexpectedly died of a sudden heart attack. I thought, well I could have told them that, as I already knew.

The striking similarity of content in both the English and American accounts have revealed an almost uniform turn of phrase to portray the very vivid visual impressions that the experience imprinted in the minds of the respondents. Words such as beauty, peace, happiness, warmth and love permeate every portrayal of the sensed events. The narratives all emphasise that the surroundings encountered are of supernal loveliness and surpass anything that can be imagined on this plane of existence. The implications are, therefore, that the journey is much the same for nearly everyone who undertakes it and that it is only different aspects that are met with along the way.

There is, however, another direction which the journey into the 'world within' may take. Although a number of noted researchers found no evidence to support this, I came across enough manifestations of hell-like experiences to rebut the theory that negative feelings are rarely, if ever, encountered. I am therefore compelled to conclude that such experiences, though infrequent, do certainly exist.

# CHAPTER 5
## *Negative near-death experiences*

Know that in whatever state you find yourself – of
mind, of body, of physical condition – that is what you
have built and is necessary for your unfoldment.
*Edgar Cayce*

In the preceding chapter I examined all the aspects of the NDE
that are included within the unfolding 'core experience', which, as
is seen, repeatedly emphasise the extremely positive and
'heavenly' nature of the encounter. I now propose to review
another aspect of the near-death phenomenon, one that is
reported to be decidedly unpleasant, namely the negative or
'hell-like' experience. While the principle emphasis in most
reports of near-death research has been on the celestial quality of
the experience, I nevertheless found indications that pointed to
the fact that negative encounters, while infrequent, do however
definitely exist.

From conversations with physicians who have recounted to me
cases of NDEs reported to them by their patients following
resuscitation from clinical death, and from my own research into
the matter, I found evidence to support the claim that negative
experiences are most likely to be obtained immediately after the
event. This is due, so it seems, to the minimal time gap between the
near-death episode itself and the procuring of the information
pertaining to it.

One cardiologist I know who is acquainted with near-death
phenomena as a result of reports he has received from his patients
over the years, told me that he believed people who had gone
through a hell-like experience were usually reluctant to disclose
the information later on, as they often felt ashamed to admit to
what had apparently happened to them. His observations have led
him to conclude that patients are more likely to volunteer the facts

while the experience is still relatively immediate. For it seems that individuals who have had a negative near-death episode can sometimes feel that the occurrence must in some way have happened because of hidden guilt feelings they are not anxious to disclose. This is in obvious contrast to the people who had experienced a positive NDE who, aside from the fear of ridicule and disbelief they were afraid their disclosures would elicit, were usually very pleased to be able to share with someone they could trust an experience they felt had immeasurably increased their feelings of confidence and self-worth.

The above comment undoubtedly bears out the argument put forward by Maurice Rawlings, whose research into negative near-death episodes is one of the few major studies that contends hellish encounters exist. This is in direct contrast to Michael Sabom, also a cardiologist, whose recent investigation reports a 'complete failure to obtain any cases suggestive of a hellish experience' and supports the position taken by Kenneth Ring. Cardiologists are, of course, among the few people who have access to patients at the time of resuscitation and are therefore in a position to carry out a prospective survey as they have no prior knowledge concerning whether or not an NDE has taken place. On the other hand, retrospective research such as my own (and for the most part that of other studies that have been carried out for the purpose of determining what takes place at the moment of apparent death) almost invariably produces positive reports, although the few cases of negative experience that I came across were reported to me some time after the event.

In attempting to follow up this aspect of NDEs (having once established the existence of the phenomenon), I found that I met with considerable resistance when attempting to reach people whose case histories were recounted to me; for, whereas doctors were often willing to discuss their patients' problems with a professional colleague, they were generally unwilling to put one in touch with them, since they were understandably reluctant to be implicated in research that the medical profession as a whole still regards as being decidedly unscientific.

As the case histories of negative experiences are, as already noted, both infrequently reported and difficult to reach, I have been obliged to draw upon those cases that have been referred to in other studies, in order to back up my own survey. There were,

at the time of my examination of the American NDEs, no case
histories in the archives of IANDS that indicated the existence of
negative or hell-like experiences. So, in order to illustrate my
respondents' accounts for the purpose of cross-cultural comparison, I will need to resort to this method to illustrate the similarity
of content, or otherwise, that was involved in the experiences of
those few individuals whose near-death episodes I have been able
to obtain by direct interview.

However, before proceeding with the respondents' narratives,
it will be necessary to clarify what is meant by a negative and what
is meant by a hell-like episode. A negative experience is usually
characterised by a feeling of extreme fear or panic. Other elements
can include emotional and mental anguish, extending to states of
the utmost desperation. People report being lost and helpless and
there is often an intense feeling of loneliness during this period
coupled with a great sense of desolation. The environment is
described as being dark and gloomy, or it can be barren and
hostile. People sometimes report finding themselves on the brink
of a pit or at the edge of an abyss, and state that they needed to
marshal all their inner resources to save themselves from plunging
over the edge. Alternatively, some people felt that they were being
tricked into death and needed to keep their wits about them to
prevent this from happening.

The hell-like experience is defined as being one which includes
all the elements comprehended in the negative phase, only more so
in that feelings are encountered with a far greater intensity. There
is often a definite sense of being dragged down by some evil force,
which is sometimes identified with the powers of darkness. At this
stage, visions or wrathful of demonic creatures that threaten or
taunt the individual are occasionally described, while others
recount being attacked by unseen beings or figures which are
often faceless or hooded. The atmosphere can either be intensely
cold or unbearably hot. It is not uncommon during this phase of
the experience to hear sounds that resemble the wailing of 'souls'
in torment, or alternatively to hear a fearsome noise like that of
maddened wild beasts, snarling and crashing about. Occasionally, respondents will report a situation that resembles the
archetypal hell in which the proverbial fire and an encounter with
the devil himself are experienced.

In general, then, as will be seen negative and hell-like

experiences seem to reveal themselves in a singular way reminiscent of many aspects of positive and heavenly NDEs. And despite the fact that my sample is small, only representing an eighth of all respondents interviewed for the purpose of this study, I feel that I discovered enough examples to have been able to establish, at the very least, that certain elements exist and are common to this phase of the experience.

## FIRST PHASE: NEGATIVE NEAR-DEATH EXPERIENCES

I will start by quoting from the accounts that contain some of the negative elements encountered within the first phase of this aspect of NDEs, in order to illustrate the impressions gained at this stage, and will conclude this chapter with excerpts taken from the hell-like experiences that provide us with the most extensive impressions of this situation. The following excerpts will, I trust, serve to demonstrate something of the affective components of this experience and are intended to convey some degree of the central tendency of these statements.

The first example is one which includes a number of the unpleasant components which are to be found within the negative reports, and while it does not specifically refer to hell, it is nonetheless an account which in my view qualifies for inclusion within this category. The respondent concerned is an Englishman who underwent an operation for the removal of a kidney at the General Hospital in Kidderminster. While under the anaesthetic he found:

> I was moving along as part of a river of sound — a constant babble of human noise, but without knowing or under-standing whether the noises were in a language or not. I felt myself sinking into and becoming part of the stream and slowly being submerged by it. A great fear possessed me as if I knew that once overcome by the evergrowing mass of noise that I would be lost. I was not aware of any physical bodies, not even my own. The stream moved on and I next became aware of a black door or opening ahead of me in the distance. I sensed that if I could reach this gate I would be safe. I cried out to be allowed to pass through. About this

time I heard one voice that I recognised, it stood out from the din around me. It was the voice of my sister calling me. Still moving along sinking into the morass of noise, still overcome with fear, I suddenly was halted as if by a barrier, and a quiet unemotional voice spoke to me: 'Not until the end.' At this point I found myself in the hospital ward and I heard myself calling out that I could not breathe. The doctor was attending me and I was given oxygen. I learnt later that my wife and family had been called to the hospital because of my condition.

In the next instance we have a case which is cited by Gallup in his recently published book *Adventures in Immortality*. It relates to an event that happened to a man who was in hospital for an operation. He is quoted as saying:

I had an operation – four and a half hours I was under, and I felt I was dying. I felt I was being tricked into death. In my mind I was fighting with faces unknown to me, and I felt that I had to have all my wits about me to keep from dying. I continued to fight for some time, but, as in a dream, which can seem hours, it might have only been seconds. I remember not breathing, and strange colours, lights and designs took shape in my brain. Later, I felt relieved and woke up in the recovery room. I had stopped breathing on the operating table and was revived, I was told. I knew I had stopped breathing and I knew I was near death, even though I was under.

When reviewing this case, Gallup states:

One might immediately say that the unknown faces around him were merely vague perceptions of the medical personnel surrounding him during the operation. Similarly, the strange colours and designs might have been due to lack of oxygen getting to his brain when he stopped breathing. The problem with this explanation is that it presupposes a fuzzy, semi-conscious state, yet this man recalls being quite lucid as he battled with whatever was trying to trick him into death. With great clarity and concentration, he fought and used his wits to keep from dying. A more likely interpretation would seem to be that he found himself on the verge of extinction;

there was some sort of volitional and personal quality in the evil that he was facing; and he realised instinctively that he had to marshal all his inner resources to fight back, to keep from going over the edge.

Similarly, in the next case, which concerns a young woman who found herself undergoing the reported experience while sustaining a difficult birth, the same awareness of battling for life was present:

I started to haemorrhage and I felt myself passing out. I next found myself out of my body standing at my head and looking down on my body which was split down the middle. On one side the medical staff were dressed in green and on the other side the identical staff were dressed in white. The white side I knew represented death and the green side life. I heard a voice clearly saying, 'You have three seconds to pull yourself back to the life side or you are dead.' I could feel this person urging me on to make a decision to fight for life. There was no sense of time, the experience felt as if it went on forever. I could feel myself wavering up and down, back and forth, as if I were being reached out for, but I couldn't see anyone. After what seemed an eternity, I could see the green side was predominating and I knew I had somehow won my battle between life and death. At this point, the white side just faded into the background and everything resumed normality. Afterwards, I was told it was a close call and they had to fight to save my life. I tried to tell the doctor about it, but he brushed it aside and said I had imagined it. I felt he was laughing at me.

A further case cited by Gallup regarding this aspect of negative experience is told about a man who on this occasion was suffering from gangrene and peritonitis as a result of an appendix problem. He recollected:

I felt like I was in a great black vacuum. All I could see was my arms hanging on to a set of parallel bars. I knew if I relaxed, my grip on life would cease. It was a complete sense of knowing that life had to be clung to. I knew without any question if I let go, I would die. The feeling of agony of hanging on only lasted a brief while.

While the cases just recounted do not actually portray scenes of the 'lower regions', they are nevertheless clearly in a dimension, while battling for life, that is decidedly negative in quality. In the episode that the young woman quoted, a presence was felt in the background, but the voice told her she had only three seconds in which to pull herself back to life. Again, there is a similarity here with the second phase of the 'core experience', when individuals find themselves out of the body and at some stage often hear a voice telling them to return. They, too, were made fully aware that failure to do so would result in death being permanent. But, although linear time is mentioned, there is also a paradox regarding the quality of timelessness, which is referred to by respondents in the positive phase as well.

Sometimes an individual does not have to make a personal effort to resist death, but instead may find himself rejected by death for certain reasons. In *Beyond Death's Door*, Maurice Rawlings gives an account of a patient who had been attacked, beaten and kicked nearly to death, who had just such an experience. While in the operating room awaiting surgery, he remembered:

> I felt the presence of something or some power and I thought, 'This is it.' Next, blackness. Time became of no more importance. Next I was drawn into total darkness. Then I stopped. It felt like a big hollow room. It seemed to be a very large space and totally dark. I could see nothing, but felt the presence of this power. I asked the power who I and who he or it was. Communication was not through talking but through a flow of energy. He answered that he was the Angel of Death. I believed him. The Angel went on to say that my life was not as it should be, that he could take me on but that I would be given a second chance, and that I was going back. The next thing I remember I was in the recovery room, back in my body. I was so taken in by this experience that I did not notice what kind of body I had, nor how much time had elapsed, it was so real – I believe it. I did not tell many people about my experience; I did not want to be considered crazy. But the encounter was very real to me, and I still believe I was with the Angel of Death.

Up to this point the accounts have been concerned with peoples' awareness of their hovering on the brink of permanent death. In the next episode, another aspect which has previously been alluded to will be examined. Here individuals may find themselves in a state where they are balanced on the verge of the 'pit of hell'. Although in both cases about to be recounted hell is specifically mentioned, I am inclined to feel that what is being experienced here is a foretaste of 'hell' rather than the lower regions as such.

This is well illustrated in the case of a woman who came close to death as a result of a very severe heat stroke:

> I was working in the nursing home where I have a part-time job. I am a partially trained nurse. I had spent the day on the beach. It was a glorious hot day, but I am used to the heat having lived in Khartoum for about sixteen years. I was in the kitchen supervising the evening suppers, when I was overcome by the heat from the aga cookers. I rushed outside the back door feeling faint and sick. I remember going down three or four steps. I don't remember falling, but the next thing that happened was that I had this experience. I found myself in a place surrounded by mist. I felt I was in hell. There was a big pit with vapour coming out and there were arms and hands coming out trying to grab mine . . . I was terrified that these hands were going to claw hold of me and pull me into the pit with them. As I lay there worrying what would happen next, an enormous lion bounded towards me from the other side and I let out a scream. I was not afraid of the lion, but I felt somehow he would unsettle me and push me into that dreadful pit. I remained in a state of semi-consciousness for about three days. I have never believed in hell, I feel God would never create such a place. But it was very hot down there and the vapour or steam was very hot. At the time I did not think very much about it, but in the intervening years I have realised both good and evil exist. The experience has transformed my life.

Another woman, who nearly died whilst having a hysterectomy, reported a very similar experience:

> I went into St Giles Hospital in London, to have an operation. Sometime while I was under the anaesthetic I

became aware that I was hovering above my body looking down at myself on the operating table. I felt very frightened and began to panic. I wondered why I was no longer in my body and thought I must be dead. I next found myself in a very frightening place, which I am sure was hell. I was looking down into a large pit, which was full of swirling grey mist and there were all these hands and arms reaching up and trying to grab hold of me and drag me in there. There was a terrible wailing noise, full of desperation. Then suddenly I found myself rushing back through this dark tunnel and I found myself back in my body in the hospital bed. As I went back into my body it felt like an elastic cord, which had been stretched to its limit and then is let go. I sort of snapped back again and everything seemed to vibrate with the impact.

In the first of the two instances just related, it would be easy to dismiss the episode on the grounds that the heat from the pit and the surrounding region must have been a vague awareness of the heat stroke the woman was suffering from; but even if that was somehow possible (despite the fact that she was verified as unconscious at the time of the incident), how is it conceivable for two totally unrelated people to have almost identical experiences while insensible, especially as the second woman's episode was derived from entirely different physical circumstances where no bodily heat was involved? A possible explanation might lie in the supposition that these women were both in a condition at that time where they were able to tune into an archetype at the level of the collective unconscious, whereby the tendency to organise experience in innately predetermined patterns operates. I will be examining this and other possibilities in the second part of this book.

In the following account a man who was being tested for angina by Maurice Rawlings collapsed and died. During the time it took to resuscitate him, he experienced the following:

It was black and there was a terrible wailing noise. There were a lot of other beings there, all wailing and full of desperation. I don't know what it was. I don't even like to think about it now because I can feel the terror again. But as far as I am concerned I was in hell.

Here again we have cross-cultural similarities in the descriptions of the wailing noise and the sense of desperation which is almost identical. In the last three accounts all the narratives reveal that the individuals who underwent the experience were aware of others down there with them, and all three quite distinctly said that without any doubt they knew that they were in hell.

I will end this phase of the accounts of negative NDEs with a case that I came across which involves a woman who was reported to have been in a coma for five days as a result of attempting to commit suicide. As the account of her episode gives such a very detailed and interesting description of the events she encountered during this time, I have decided to include it here as I feel it is of great interest. Although the experience is obviously negative, in some respects it also contains definite elements that are usually associated with positive NDEs. I was not able to verify the facts, so I can only relate the account as a means of reinforcing what has been related so far. I wish to point out that this story is in no way intended to be taken as part of my sample of respondents.

In the narrative that was related this woman evidently insisted that the experiences 'were not dreams or hallucinations. A dream is often nebulous, but what I saw and heard were of an incredible clarity. Even after five years I remember perfectly all the details.' She evidently woke in a world of silence, convinced she had done something harmful to herself. She then went on to say: 'I had a certainty of not dreaming but of being conscious of myself, my thoughts, sentiments and sensations.' She next found herself in a dark room. Slowly, as she grew used to the twilight, she realised that she was lying on a cold marble table. She said: 'I sought some sound, the presence of someone. But I was alone, desolately alone. I waited for something, anything, not to remain in the state of mental anguish that grew and grew.' She then seems to have found herself in a spacious, though austere chapel, which she felt was a kind of hospital. Suddenly, she became aware of a dazzling light at her feet, which came from a beautiful gold lantern on a stand about six feet high. Its white light shone directly on her. She remembers thinking: 'My God, how cold it is am I alive or dead? A dead person would have flowers, someone there who wept. But, if I am alive, I shall certainly die if no one helps me.' She recalls her feelings at that time, which were a mixture of indignation at being left alone and fear of the unknown. Presently she saw a male figure, young, pale, with dark eyes, which were fixed understandingly on her. She tried to communicate mentally with him and he answered in the same fashion. She called: 'Help me, help me, whoever you are.' He responded: 'Be calm and have faith.' She next became conscious of the sounds of voices which grew louder and louder. At the same time she noticed that there was a spiral staircase which led upwards. She mentally saw the upper floor which was an austere, whitewashed room like a convent. Figures in dark cloaks were conversing – discussing her. They were figures without faces – or at any rate their cloaks hid their features. She knew that she was 'being tried, accused of having transgressed and would have to pay'. She recalls that although several speakers defended her, a greater number accused her. She was terrified, but says that the 'being of light gave me courage and made me understand that it would be unjust if they condemned me and he would stop them if they did'. The next thing that happened was that suddenly there was a violent slamming of a door, following by a tramping of feet, as if people were hurrying. The staircase creaked under the weight of a multitude who burst into the room. There were many dark figures who were old and bent. She continued: 'They fell upon me. I hardly had time to throw a last entreating glance at the being of light. I felt the judgment was that they had condemned me.' But when the crowd tried to seize her they were unable to advance. She said: 'I escaped their hands because the light stopped them a few centimetres from me. They withdrew and I knew I was absolved.' She ended her account by saying: 'Was it the judgment I feared? Or perhaps I feared not saving my soul. I saw that to cut oneself off from life was indeed a mortal sin.' When she regained consciousness, though her body felt 'light, restored and physically well' during her experience, she was surprised to find that she was in fact uncomfortable with tubes and catheters sticking out of her.

What makes this account so interesting, apart from the fact that it is very detailed and explicit, is that it cuts across so many of the assumptions made to date about near-death episodes. First, as can be seen from this report, elements of both a negative and a positive nature are present. While the woman was quite clearly in a negative environment, she nevertheless had the protection, support and encouragement of the 'being of light', which is usually associated with positive experiences, to sustain her long ordeal. Another interesting fact concerns the judgment she was subjected to. In all the 'core experiences', respondents quite categorically state that there was no sense of judgment, that any judgment came from themselves. Furthermore, although the condition that brought about her NDE, an attempt to take her own life, seems to have been the reason for her finding herself in the circumstances that she did, this is another unusual aspect that contradicts much of what has been established so far. Kenneth Ring found that attempted suicides were less likely than others to have a full 'core experience'. He draws attention to the fact that a 'most striking feature of suicide-related near-death experiences, one that sets them apart from the prototypical episode, is the total absence of stages IV and V'. He goes on to say that among would-be suicides in his study no one ever reported seeing 'a brilliant but comforting light, or encountered a presence'. He further states that a sense of bodily detachment exists to the same degree as other categories but that even if it gets this far at all it usually ends with a 'feeling of confused drifting in a dark or murky void – a sort of "twilight zone", which simply tends to fade out before the "transcendent elements" characteristic of the 'core experience' make their appearance'. Finally, while the data on failed suicides was inconclusive, as he makes clear, the basic findings, however, did suggest a 'possible departure from the invariance hypothesis', in that the NDEs appeared to be 'aborted or truncated' as compared to other categories of near-death survival. Furthermore, it was found that the clearest suicide recall was associated with cases that did not entail the use of drugs.

But what do other well-known studies have to say about this aspect? According to Raymond Moody, while he has recently stated that 'in the mass of material I have collected no one has ever described to me a state like the archetypal hell', he has also previously asserted in his book *Life After Life* that these experiences were uniformly characterised as being unpleasant. He evidently found that what suicide-related near-death experiences revealed was that the conflicts that these people had attempted to escape from by this method were still present when they died. They further differed from the experiences of others whose NDEs had been brought about through illness or accident, in that they found their complications had the added disadvantage that in their disembodied state they were unable to do anything about their problems and were obliged to view 'the unfortunate consequences which resulted from their acts'. To illustrate his point, Dr Moody gives an example of this by referring to a man who, because he was despondent about the death of his wife, shot himself and 'died' as a result. But before being resuscitated he found: 'I didn't go where [my wife] was. I went to an awful place . . . I immediately saw the mistake I had made . . .I thought, "I wish I hadn't done it." ' Dr Moody further adds that:

> Others who experienced this unpleasant 'limbo' state have remarked that they had the feeling they would be there for a long time. This was their penalty for 'breaking the rules' by trying to release themselves prematurely from what was, in effect, an 'assignment' – to fulfil a certain purpose of life.

This sentiment has also been expressed by a number of people who had 'core experiences' who said that while they were near death it was communicated to them that suicide is an act against God, that all life is sacred, that to take the life of oneself or another is attended with very severe penalties.

So far the accounts have brought us to the threshold of the second stage of these experiences. From this point on, hell is no longer sensed as being an imminent danger; instead, it becomes the preternatural inferno which engulfs the individual:

## SECOND PHASE: HELL-LIKE NEAR-DEATH EXPERIENCES

I will now move on to the second phase of this expression of NDEs and examine those accounts which give us the most extensive perspectives of this phase of the phenomenon.

A man who was suffering from TB testified that, during his stay in the nursing home where he was being treated, he one day had an overwhelming urge to end his life by throwing himself out of the window:

> I felt an inner struggle going on between myself and some evil force. At the last moment I suddenly felt an inner explosion and seemed to be enveloped in a blue flame which felt cold. At this point I found myself floating about six

inches above my body. The next thing I remember is being sucked down a vast black vortex like a whirlpool and I found myself in a place that I can only describe as being like Dante's *Inferno*. I saw a lot of other people who seemed grey and dreary and there was a musty smell of decay. There was an overwhelming feeling of loneliness about the place.

The next excerpt, which comes from another case related by Maurice Rawlings, concerns a man who 'died' for an hour following an accident at a timber conveyor. It has a number of similarities with the example that has just been cited. It is quoted below:

I remember more clearly than any other thing that has ever happened to me in my lifetime, every detail of every moment, what I saw and what happened during that hour I was gone from the world. I was standing some distance from this burning, turbulent, rolling mass of blue fire. . . . I saw other people I had known that had died. . . . We recognised each other, even though we did not speak. Their expressions were those of bewilderment and confusion. The scene was so awesome that words simply fail. There is no way to escape, no way out. You don't even try to look for one. This is the prison out of which no one can escape except by Divine Intervention.

And from a further patient of Maurice Rawlings, who nearly died from an inflammatory condition of the pancreas, comes this account:

I was going through this long tunnel and I was wondering why my feet weren't touching the sides. I seemed to be floating and going very fast. It seemed to be underground. It may have been a cave, but the awfullest, eery sounds were going on. There was an odour of decay like a cancer patient would have. Everything now seemed to be in slow motion. I can't recall all of the things I saw, but some of the workers were only half human, mocking and talking to each other in a language I didn't understand. . . . I don't remember leaving there or how I got back. There are a lot of other things that may have happened that I don't remember. Maybe I'm afraid to remember.

Again, as in the case of positive experiences, a number of similar components are present. There is an awareness of being out of the body and also the sense of travelling through black space at great speed which assumes the shape of a vast black vortex like a whirlpool; the difference being that in this instance the individual has a definite feeling of going down instead of up. Both the British and American respondents describe the flame or fire as being blue in colour, just as some of the positive experiencers have described the light as being blue. Both also refer to an unpleasant odour of decay and the atmosphere portrayed is one of loneliness and desolation in each case. With positive experiences, too, occasionally a sense of smell can be involved, but then the person will become aware of a delightful fragrance which has been likened to the scent of flowers or can again sometimes resemble incense.

Another instance of this feeling of fear and coldness, accompanied by dreadful noises, came from a man who had a cardiac arrest. He said:

> I was going down, deep down into the earth. There was anger and I felt this horrible fear. Everything was grey. The noise was fearsome, with snarling and crashing like maddened wild animals, gnashing their teeth. I knew where I was without having to ask. I was in hell. There was this terrible feeling of being lost. It wasn't all fire and brimstone like we were taught. I remember this feeling of coldness. There were other things there whirling about. And there were two beings of some kind near me. I believe one was evil, maybe the Devil. He was the force that was tugging me deeper and deeper down into that awful place. I felt enveloped by dark, black evil. I remember frantically trying to put this two-piece puzzle together. I had to get it done or suffer some terrible, nameless punishment. You don't hear any words, you sense it all. Well, there was no way this puzzle would fit and I remember being in a panic. The other being I'm sure now was Jesus. I remember somehow knowing that He could save me. I tried to shout His name but I couldn't, there was this screaming in my head. Then I felt I was rushing through that black void again. I opened my eyes and my wife and the doctors were leaning over me, telling me everything was going to be alright.

So far the experiences we have described, while being nightmarish, are still not exactly in line with the concept of 'burning forever in the fires of hell'. (In fact a number of the accounts have referred to the feeling of coldness that pervades the atmosphere.) So, are there any reports that give an account of anything approaching a full-scale hell-fire scenario? Again, I have to refer to Maurice Rawlings to give us an example. This account concerns a woman who had attempted to commit suicide by taking an overdose of Valium while in a state of despondency:

> As I got drowsy, I remember going down this black hole, round and round. Then I saw a glowing red-hot spot getting bigger and bigger until I was able to stand up. It was all red and hot and on fire. The earth was like slimy mud that sank over my feet and it was hard to breathe. I cried out, 'Oh Lord, give me another chance.' I prayed and prayed. How I got back I'll never know. They said I was unconscious for two days and that they pumped my stomach. They said my experience in hell must have been a drug trip. But they don't really know. I've taken Valium many times before, but never had an experience with it.

Before concluding this chapter I will add just one more experience that was reported in 'The Evergreen Study', which was published in *Anabiosis – The Journal for Near-Death Studies*. The researchers report that they came across only one case involving 'hell-fire and damnation' in their investigation. What follows here is an abridged version of their transcript.

> I went downstairs! Downstairs was dark, people were howling [there was] fire, they wanted a drink of water. . . . First we went down . . . it was pitchblack. It was not a tunnel, more than a tunnel, a great big one. I was floating down. . . . I seen a lot of people down there, screaming, howling. . . . No clothes at all . . . you can't count them . . . I'd say about almost a million to me. . . . They were miserable and hateful. They were asking me for water. They didn't have any water . . . he was there. He had his little horns on . . . I'd know him anywhere. . . . The devil himself.

The interview evidently continued with descriptions of the heat and fire of hell, the devil's disciples and the time the respondent spent there (about four hours). We have thus penetrated about as far on this journey to the lower realms as these reports will take us. In the second part of this book I will be discussing the implications inherent in the experience to see what lessons can be learnt from these extraordinary accounts.

As the foregoing passages have shown, these testimonies reveal certain similarities of content that have shown themselves to be present in heavenly episodes. Like those respondents who had positive experiences, the people in this category returned from their encounter with an increased conviction that life continues after death. They also felt a strong urge radically to modify their former way of life. It would therefore seem that the outcome of the investigation into these negative near-death perspectives has disclosed that this aspect not only contains a number of similarities associated with the 'core experience', but also (interestingly enough) includes a set of elements with a prevailing sequence of events that are congruous with them as well. These categories can be summed up as follows:

1  Fear and a feeling of panic
2  Out-of-the-body experience
3  Entering a black void
4  Sensing an evil force
5  Entering a hell-like environment.

Five people I interviewed claimed to have had a terrifying experience; one respondent had a hell-like experience on one near-death occasion, and a positive 'core experience' subsequently. Since altogether about an eighth of my respondents reported experiences that were hell-like, this corresponds more closely with the findings of Maurice Rawlings and George Gallup rather than with those of Kenneth Ring and Michael Sabom. The reasons for this discrepancy remain to be elucidated.

# CHAPTER 6
# *Subjective perceptions of near-death experiences*

> Authentic symbolism is present when something
> specific represents something more universal, not as a
> dream or a shadow, but as a living momentary
> revelation of what is inscrutable.
>
> *Goethe*

During the course of examining both positive and negative
near-death episodes, I have touched upon a number of remarkable
phenomenological features that cut across the phases of the NDE
and bring them to a conclusion. As these elements are among the
most singular of the ones to be found within the NDE, I now
propose to examine them in a separate chapter in order to take a
deeper look at what they convey.

These elements occur when the dying have arrived at the point
where they seem to have reached the 'borderland' of another
realm of existence, but while the possibility still remains of
reversing the process of death. Awareness of reaching this point of
resolution is usually determined by the manifestation of one of
several characteristics. Although it will be necessary to take them
in some sort of chronological order, the impression that one gains
from the narratives of the respondents when they are relating this
phenomenon is that in fact these features frequently happen in no
definite sequence, but rather seem mostly to occur as a
simultaneous matrix of impressions.

In Table 2, I have indicated the five principal features which
were arrived at during the process of compiling my original
research material.

In discussing this border or limit in *Life After Life*, Raymond
Moody, when referring to this feature, suggests:

73

TABLE 2

The five phenomenological features encountered at the 'boundary' (reached by thirty-two subjects).

| The boundary | No. |
| --- | --- |
| Some kind of barrier | 2 |
| The 'presence' | 3 |
| Meeting with deceased 'spirits' | 10 |
| Life review | 10 |
| Decision to return | 17 |

One could raise the question of whether there might not be some one basic experience or idea at the root of all of them. If this is true then the different versions would merely represent varying individual ways of interpreting, wording, or remembering the root experience.

In the next section I will be considering some accounts of this feature in order to see what purpose this aspect fulfils.

## THE BOUNDARY

At some stage in their passage towards apparent death respondents do sometimes state that they find themselves halted by some sort of barrier which impedes their progress and prevents them from going on. It subsequently transpires that if they were allowed to continue, their journey would ultimately lead to irreversible death. The barrier, which usually manifests during this phase, can be a tangible obstacle or an invisible wall which they come up against; but whatever form it takes, it invariably has the effect of reversing the process that their near-death crisis initiated.

When they reach the threshold of the 'inner world' they can either be faced with a river that they are unable to cross, a door through which they are not permitted to pass, or the object can be any other kind of impediment that bars their passage and marks the boundary between the borderland and the 'celestial realms' beyond. In the excerpts that follow, instances where this limit was reached will be related, so as to give an idea of the kind of patterned coherence attending this phenomenon.

It may be recalled that one of the British respondents, who had temporarily died of a cardiac arrest during an operation, recollected that she was not allowed to cross the threshold and enter the house in which her mother could be seen. When she pleaded, 'Can I come in?' her mother said, 'No, you can't, it's not your time to stay.' A similar incident was reported by a man whose near-death episode has not been previously mentioned. He 'died' several times before the electric shock treatment he was being given to restart his heart functioning became effective. Upon recovery he reported, 'I saw a door in a wall of the garden. Behind the door was a long corridor. I was very much aware that whatever happened I must not get to the end of that corridor.' While another man who was in intensive care following an almost fatal fall found himself confronted by 'a large white illuminated door. As I started to go through the door there was a flash of light like the afterglow of lightning and I woke up in hospital.' And for another heart attack victim it happened this way:

> Before me there seemed to be a dark curtain that I felt would shortly open. I knew I was on the threshold of a new and wonderful experience. I looked forward to it with anticipation, feeling that I could hardly wait for it to begin. Then suddenly I was back again in my body. I don't know how.

Sometimes it is an invisible barrier of attachment that prevents individuals from continuing on their jounrey, such as the memory of loved ones from whom they cannot bear the thought of being parted. This was the case with the woman whose NDE I cited earlier to illustrate the light. She said in response to this feature: 'I felt I couldn't go forward because I wanted to see my children and my husband again.' In one of the American instances something similar happened involving a person of whom the respondent was extremely fond, but in this case it was the person who had been 'left behind' who urged his return:

> I really didn't want to leave this condition at all, it was Jerry's insistence that I take his hand. Jerry is my friend and priest. His hand was extended down the tube [tunnel] and he wanted me to take his hand. This stood out above all other things in my mind. Jerry was not actually in the room

at the time, he had been there and he had given me the last
rites and we had parted on the insistence of the doctors. I
was very comfortable and did not want to come back. I felt I
had reached a wonderful place that I never wanted to leave.
But Jerry seemed to be sort of pleading with me. He wanted
me to take his hand. It was extended or elongated up the
tube to me. He seemed to be wanting my survival. Even my
wife's distress – she was not actually in the room but sort of
outside – even that was not enough to make me want to
come back. It was Jerry's insistence.

The last two examples quoted really overlap in a number of
instances with the final stage that occurs during this phase of the
experience, which is the decision to return. But, as I have already
stressed, it is very difficult to separate the different elements, even
though it has been necessary to list them in a certain order. For not
only do they intermingle with one another, but, as I have
previously pointed out, respondents frequently mention that these
features appear to function like a hologram; that is to say,
everything seems to be happening simultaneously.


## THE PRESENCE

Some respondents report that during this phase they become
aware of a 'presence'. Communication may be by way of mental
understanding or may take the form of a voice which is heard to
speak; but whatever the medium, the message that is conveyed is
always clearly to inform individuals that this is the point where
they must make a decision regarding their future. At times this
presence can be experienced in association with the barrier and at
others it is encountered independently. Sometimes the presence is
sensed but not seen, while on other occasions it can be seen as a
radiant light which is felt to be the source of universal light and
enlightenment. For others, again, the presence may appear to take
the form of Jesus or some religious figure to whom the individual
is attached. Respondents often claim to be aware of having a very
special relationship to this presence which is sometimes
understood to be God, and at times is felt to be the higher self of
the indivdiual. Very often these two are perceived to be one and

the same and people frequently stress that there is, in reality, no separation from God. As one respondent said, 'I feel that this is what Jesus must have meant when he said, "I and my Father are One".'

The next excerpt, while containing a number of comparable similarities with the last two instances quoted in the previous section, leads us on to the ensuing components by virtue of the presence of Jesus being mentioned. In this regard I return again to the case of the man who found himself in the mortuary upon returning to his body. In answer to the question, 'How were you revived?' he had this to say:

> Well, again, in this state I heard as it were a whisper, which got louder and louder, of an elderly woman's voice [his old landlady] praying, 'O God, don't let him die, he's got a work to do for you.' This grated and I didn't like it at all, and the Lord Jesus turned me round on my shoulder and gave me a gentle push and said something to the effect of, 'It's not time for you yet', and I woke up in the mortuary.

As well as providing a link with the voice heard praying for his return, this quote also corresponds with the next citation where a feeling that one is being physically turned round and pushed back is also reported. The woman who had a bad allergic reaction to drugs remembered:

> I wanted to stay forever, but I felt someone very strong put their hand on my shoulders and turn me round. I knew I had to go back and I was dreadfully disappointed. But although there were no words, I knew I was being told 'Not yet'.

Whereas in the case of the woman who had a very difficult time giving birth, it was a man's voice that she heard commanding, 'You must go back. Remember the baby. Who's going to look after it? You must go back.'

Others, again, may not see or hear anything, but a 'presence' is distinctly felt which communicates with the person concerned. The content of the message received, though, is always to issue the same injunction, namely that the individual must return. This was the case with one of the respondents whose NDE resulted from a heart attack. She put her experience this way:

I was up, and although I didn't see anything there was a presence and it was like maybe not really talking to me, but knew what was going on. It wasn't like his telling me that I had to go down, but it was like I knew I had to go down and I didn't want to, yet I wanted to. It was like being pulled, without being pulled, my feelings were I guess being pulled apart. I was not afraid to go that way. I really wanted to go there, something was there. I shall always remember that, and I had no fear of it. The peace, the release, the fear was all gone, the pain there was nothing, it was absolutely beautiful, I could never explain it in a million years, but it was a feeling that everybody dreams of someday having. Peace is the only word I can use to express it, it means so much to me, and joy. I wanted to go that way, but I had to go back. I feel I made a choice, I was drawn back. I wasn't afraid to go that way, and yet, I felt it was my choice to go back. I think I had to come back because I had two little children and I felt they needed me, more than up there where I felt it was my peace and joy, but it meant misery for my children. I feel even then I was weighing these things; I wasn't feeling any pain or sorrow, but I was thinking calmly and rationally, making a logical decision without emotions involved. As a mother we are ruled mostly by emotion, but I did not make an emotional decision, I made it logically and the choice was mine. I felt the presence was with me all the time and it was communicating with me, not through speaking, but I was aware of the decision that I had to make; I knew to stay meant that I would die, but I was never afraid at any time.

This feeling of emotional detachment is often mentioned by respondents, usually with some surprise at finding that they were able to take a disinterested view of their loved ones without experiencing any feelings of guilt. A woman whose NDE resulted from haemorrhaging after an operation to remove fibroids in her womb, put it: 'I remember thinking that I was not worried about my daughter, which was strange, because normally she is the first person I worry about.'

At times the 'presence' is replaced by the 'spirits' of deceased loved ones, usually relations, but sometimes dear friends who, in contrast to unrecognisable presences, can be clearly seen and identified.

## MEETINGS WITH DECEASED 'SPIRITS'

One of the most noticeable differences between the encounters that take place with the 'presence' and the ones that occur with deceased 'spirits' is that while the former appears to encourage people to decide for themselves, the latter, while greeting the individuals in a loving manner, almost always serve to remind them that it is not time for them to stay, and that they must 'go back'. Whatever the case may be, the stage has now been reached when the decision whether or not to return has to be made, and which in some cases involves being reluctantly sent back.

In the next excerpt one of the respondents who suffered a heart attack said:

> I saw my parents approaching me. They appeared as I always remember them to be, in fact they looked as if they were waiting for me and expecting me. I remember them putting their hands out to me and saying, 'We've been waiting for you.'

While another heart attack victim found:

> There was my father standing before me as large as life. He had died of a heart attack fifteen years before. He was dressed just like he used to be in grey trousers and a cardigan. He hadn't changed a bit. We chatted quite naturally and he joked with me about my brothers.

The woman who had two major operations in two days said of this aspect:

> Before my sense of awe turned into fear, my sister [who was killed in 1949, aged 20] appeared, a woman of 43; but her face had no lines of physical life and her smile was joyous. My awe became delight; 'Mary Elizabeth', I said, 'I am so happy to be here!' 'I know', she answered, 'but you can't stay. You must go back to your five reasons.' With that she

brought my five children in turn, naming each one. I was
overwhelmed. I had no choice. I was being wrenched away –
I was angry – I was back. . . . I was alive and with the will to
live, in the knowledge of a renewed sense of life and a
heightened understanding of what we call death.

And from a man who had a nearly fatal fall came this quote: 'I saw
my father who had died a couple of years before. It was just as if I
had seen him last week.' A woman who collapsed and nearly died
when her heart stopped beating had the following experience
while she was being rushed by ambulance to hospital:

Inside the cottage I found my mother and father and my
grandparents. My daughter who had also passed on was
there too. I asked them where I was and what I was doing
there. They told me I was in the spirit world. When I asked if
I was there to stay, my father said, 'It's not yet time for you
to join us.'

Occasionally, people will meet up with deceased relatives
whose death was not previously known to them, only to find
subsequently that the person concerned has indeed died. It may be
recalled that this was the case with the woman whose cardiac
arrest resulted in her finding herself on the threshold of her
mother's prefabricated house, but who was not allowed to enter.
She was told in response to her observation that they 'seemed to be
expecting someone', that they were indeed getting ready for the
imminent arrival of a relative. She was not surprised, therefore, to
learn upon recovery that the relative in question had unexpectedly
died of a sudden heart attack during the time that she was in
intensive care. This very provocative element of the near-death
episode also sometimes works the other way round in that people
will meet up with a long dead relation who was unknown to them
prior to their near-death encounter, only later to come across a
picture of him or her which they instantly recognise as being the
image of the person whom they had met while 'on the other side'.

A case in point concerns a young girl who 'died' for almost
twenty minutes when she was a child, as a result of a brain virus.
After she recovered she described her 'journey to the stars'.
Recently she said:

I can remember it all even though it was a long time ago. I

was in a big garden. I could see a stream and trees laden with pomegranates. It was extremely bright and there were people there. One was my grandfather. There was his mother too. She took me in her lap and kissed me. I can remember hearing my father asking me to come back. My grandfather asked me what I wanted to do and I told him I wanted to be with my father. He said I would have to ask God. Holding his hand we went to see Him and all I remember about Him was brightness and light. The next thing I knew, I was on my bed with both my parents there.

Sometime later, when visiting a relative's house, her parents were amazed when she recognised a photograph of her great grandmother standing on a dresser. She pointed it out and said, 'That's the lady I saw and that's my grandfather.' Both had died long before she was born and she had never seen either of them.

Another aspect which can often be decisive in helping to resolve the dilemma facing the individual at this point, regarding whether or not they should remain 'in heaven' or return to complete an earthly life, is the life review.

## THE LIFE REVIEW

This feature can occur at any time during the phase of experiencing the more transcendental elements associated with the 'borderland', and usually involves the sudden occurrence of a very rapid review of the individual's life up to that point. This may include entire or partial aspects of a person's existence prior to the near-death event, generally seen as instantaneous and vivid visual images. These images appear in no definite sequence, although in some cases they do, and can in some instances include precognition of coming events, which are either personal or may involve global issues. This re-experiencing of their life's events usually has the effect of causing people to reflect on what has happened up to that point and gives them an opportunity to reassess their former values.

The account given below comes from one of the people who suffered a heart attack. It is another of those instances where it is difficult to know which category it fits into, as prior to the experience recounted here the respondent had been describing a 'beautiful presence'. He recalled that as he became aware of it,

> This radiation of love entered me and instantly I was part of it or it was a part of me. There was instant communication. My entire life was, snap, like that, [he snapped his fingers here to illustrate his point] things that, I mean, He, God – I'm not afraid to call him that – knew: everything, right off the bat. I felt ashamed, I was ashamed of certain things that I had done in my life that I knew were wrong, and yet things that I had completely forgotten about I was made cognisant of and these were the things that were important; like when I was a kid, say eighteen or nineteen years old, I worked on a tubercular survey for school children and this was good. You know, I'd forgotten all about it, I'd only done this for a couple of years; these things just came back, I was instantly told everything. I was encompassed by the greatest feeling of love there possibly is, there are no words, it was instant communication.

And for the man who had a nearly fatal fall the 'presence' is also referred to in the following incident, in relation to the life review and the command that he should return:

> My life started to flash before me. I felt embarrassed every time a stupid thing I had done came up. I sensed that the 'presence' was saying, 'Yes, you did these things, but you were learning at the same time.' It was then communicated to me that I should now go back. I didn't want to, but I understood that there was still a lot of work for me to do.

While for the man who 'died' of pleurisy and pneumonia it may be remembered how 'The pieces of the jigsaw all fitted together. Suddenly I saw how all my life fitted together to that point.'

If the life review gives people an opportunity to take a detached look at the incidents that have occurred in their lives so far, the next phase, which is the decision to return, affords them the chance to 'come back' and live their lives with their changed perspectives.

## THE DECISION TO RETURN

However the individuals feel the decision to return was made, the vital issue really seems to concern the need to 'come back' in order to complete their allotted span on earth, so as to have an opportunity of accomplishing their life-tasks before being cut off from this possibility, as would be the case if they were allowed to remain. Whether they decided to return or were sent back, the reason invariably has to do with either a consideration for the suffering of the people that are left behind and the difficulties that will be experienced in their lives as a result of the person's death, or a feeling that the purpose of the individual's life has not yet been fulfilled and that they need to return to complete their intended design. In almost all cases, whether the choice is an individual one or is impressed upon them, the motivation for the decision to return would seem to be a sense of mission and service to God and mankind, selfless love and consideration for others. In all events, reaching a decision to return is the final event in the process and one which appears to reverse the passage of dying and returns the individual to the world of ordinary reality. In the illustrations that ensue I will give examples of the features just described.

The next three accounts all come from respondents who had heart attacks. All have been mentioned before at one time or another. The first quote comes from one of the American NDErs:

> I suddenly stopped [going towards the luminous being] and I was given a choice, although it wasn't really a choice, to go on or go back. I went through the agony of making that decision and I was writhing mentally. There was no physical pain whatsoever; the nearest I can come to it is if you have ever gone fishing and you put a worm on a hook and you see it wriggling. Well, that was what my spirit was doing. I was writhing, I was in torture, like backwards and forward. What shall I do? Well, I thought of the things that I hadn't done. I was worried about my wife taking care of things and I decided or was permitted to return. So I withdrew. I still seemed to be in a physical shape. It's hard to say what this shape is, but I was there, but really not in the same physical sense. I withdrew and I guess I came back at that point. I

knew nothing more until I opened my eyes and I was in the intensive care unit. But I wanted to go back, I felt cheated, I was losing all this love.

The following excerpt is the continuation of the narrative that was given by the English psychotherapist from London:

I then understood that I had the choice of continuing or going back. This sounds like a journey, but it wasn't like that. Again, it was an understanding that to go back I had to accept the pain that I knew would be there. I realised that if I followed the light that I would not come back, but at the same time I was the light. So if I followed or surrendered to the light I would go one way, but if I fought the pain it would be unbearable. I knew I had to find a middle way and accept the pain in order to come back. But it was very much a choice. I felt I could have gone the way of the light, but at the same time I had a feeling – this is very hard to put into words – that I was not ready to go.

The third statement comes from another of the American respondents:

Suddenly I was communicated to by someone, possibly my father, that I must come back, that it was not time for me, that there was much that I had to do and that I had to return. I know that I didn't feel the sadness, or not that I can describe, it was not the kind of feeling that I would feel in this consciousness, just a wanting to stay and knowing that I could not, must not stay. I felt a tremendous pain, a wrenching pain that seemed to tear every bit of my body; a pain that I have never felt before and I will never forget. I also seemed to see surrounding me tremendous electrical impulses, great shocks, which I can only describe as electrical impulses.

Finally, the English woman who had a virus infection in the spinal cord gave this account of what she experienced during this phase:

Then I noticed that there were three figures slightly above me. They appeared to be Indian as their skin was light brown. They were clad in some silvery, metallic looking robes, with turbans of the same colour on their heads. All three had a jewel, or eye, in the middle of their foreheads which was emitting a ray of light. We did not speak, but somehow I understood that a decision was being made regarding whether I was to be allowed to stay or whether I was to be sent back. Suddenly I found myself rushing back down a long dark tunnel. I could see a light at the end and also my daughter's face peering anxiously down.

This narrative concludes the reports that relate to the unfolding phases of the NDE. As the events just described have clearly shown, whatever the interpretation one puts on these experiences, the individuals concerned unquestionably felt the surroundings that they found themselves in were real and vastly superior to the world of everyday experience, and one can readily understand why such a person entering this realm would be reluctant to return. With these descriptions of this phase of the NDE, I have followed the phenomenological path of the dying as far as these accounts will allow. But before I move on to an examination of the after-effects that this extraordinary experience has on its recipients, there are a number of features that require clarification.

## CONCLUSIONS

Now that all of the experiences reported by the respondents have been presented, it has become evident that they appear to follow a certain progression. The reader may well be wondering what the characteristic features associated with the phenomenon are. So I feel that a brief summary of these issues is called for before concluding this part of the book.

From the accounts just related, what has clearly emerged is that a common pattern of events, involving a sequence of occurrences that seem to be almost universal in their conformity of content, are conspicuous characteristic of NDEs. The sequential features of the experience have generally shown that the earlier phases are inclined to be more frequent, while the latter phases manifest less frequently. This conclusion would therefore tend to bear out Kenneth Ring's contention that not only are some categories more common than others, but also that they appear in a decreasing order of frequency.

Among the principal factors that need to be clarified, a number of qualitative elements call for an explanation. These aspects have already been identified by several other researchers, so I will not be discussing them here at any length; but as this is a comparative study a short review of the relative findings is necessary to show the conformity of content.

## Dream interpretation

A question frequently asked is how closely NDEs resemble a dream. While this can never be decisively settled the overwhelming majority of respondents in answer to this inquiry emphatically deny any correspondence to the dream state and insist instead that it was real.

## Hallucinations as a cause

The question of the possibility of the NDE being a hallucination is another related supposition. While some evidence does exist for the occurrence of hallucinatory type images among NDErs, in almost every case these images were recognised to have been hallucinations. The following instance was reported by a psychotherapist with a professional knowledge of both dreams and hallucinations and what he said typically illustrates this point:

> The experience I had was totally real, it was definitely not anything like a dream, nor was it like the detached feeling you get during a hallucination on LSD, where there is a dream-like quality of watching yourself, but not really being part of what is going on. That's more like watching yourself on a TV screen. But I was really experiencing what was happening to me and was not even aware I was out of my body at the time. When I took LSD in the past, I experienced going into a black hole and was able with intellectual choice to stop going through. In the case of the NDE the decision was made with my whole being.

In *Life at Death*, Kenneth Ring gives an example of a similar view, which is cited by a respondent who was also a psychiatrist. She is quoted as saying that without qualification, in her judgment, her own experience was neither a dream nor a hallucination. The difference seems to lie in the fact that chemically induced visions are contrived, whereas the NDE is a spontaneous occurrence that leaves one free to choose the most creative way of responding to the situation. In discussing this point with the psychotherapist quoted above, after I had taken down the statement just related, he said:

> It is a great relief to be able to discuss my experience with someone who understands what I am saying. As near as I can get it, I would agree with you that LSD inferferes with free will, whereas in an NDE one is totally free.

This sense of relief at being able to discuss their experience without fear of ridicule and disbelief was echoed many times by other respondents during the time I was researching my case studies, and indeed continues to be the case. Whenever I give a public talk or a workshop on the subject, almost always someone will come up to me afterwards and say; 'I have never told anyone this before, but I had an experience just like the ones you have just described and I didn't want to let anyone know as I thought they would think I was going a bit peculiar.' In addition to the sense of isolation voiced by respondents, the majority also encountered the greatest difficulty in putting into adequate words the quality and depth of the experience.

### Bodily sense

If individuals are apparently aware of leaving their bodies during the time that they are evidently 'clinically dead', are they generally aware of having another body? For many respondents the answer is they are not. The people who come within this group were conscious of existing as 'mind and eyes' only. But there were also a number who were aware that they continued to be in a 'second body', which some described as an 'etheric double'. On these occasions the other body is always seen as vigorous and restored, regardless of the condition of the body that has just been vacated.

If a limb has been amputated, then the 'etheric double' is seen to be whole, or, as a woman who had been badly scarred as a result of a serious abdominal operation said, 'I was naked and I had no scars on my body.' In other instances people who were old and infirm were said to 'somehow combine the youth and vigour of a twenty-one-year-old' again. ˙

Lastly, there is the issue of the so-called 'silver cord' which is such a well-known phenomenon in the literature of parapsychology. This cord or thread is said to connect the two bodies. In two instances this manifestation was reported. In the first, the man who found himself in the mortuary when he returned to his body said:

> It was almost as if a cord linked myself to my body on the bed and I couldn't go. I thought I was caught there, and then it seemed as if the cord was severed and I arrived at this place.

The second instance was related by a woman who had a negative experience. She said:

> As I went back into my body it felt like an elastic cord, which has been stretched to its limit and then is let go. I sort of snapped back again and everything seemed to vibrate with the impact.

From the evidence it would appear, therefore, that in the earlier phases of the NDE people are generally not aware of having another body, while in the deeper NDEs the reverse is more likely to be the case, and in a small percentage of people the connecting cord was experienced.

### Cognitive and sensory processes

Respondents reported that, once detachment from the body occurred, they also became emotionally detached. Although they were conscious of having left the body, for many a state of dual awareness seemed to exist. During this phase, they also realised that at the same time a heightened intellectual process was taking place which included clearer and sharper perception. Decisions regarding their resolutions to continue with their lives on earth seemed typically to be made in this state of exalted mental clarity and detached rationality. This enhanced cognitive process was in most cases accompanied by an increased clarity of sensory perception, which was described as being both acute and precise. It seems that as the bodily sensations, e.g. pain, cease, so the sense of sight and sound become more penetrating.

As I have previously mentioned, a number of respondents alluded to the fact that time and space no longer seemed to be a reality, and that a radical transformation of perception seemed to take place.

## Gender and mode of near-death

My study was designed to investigate three distinct types of near-death onset: illness, accident and suicide attempt. The reason for the disproportionate number of accident victims, as compared to those of illness, is due to the fact that only those respondents whose accidents were unconnected with illness were included in this category. I decided not to include haemorrhaging, adverse reaction to drugs or anaesthetics etc., if connected with illness in that list.

This information is given in Table 3, which shows the percentage of people who had any kind of NDE according to sex and mode of near-death.

TABLE 3
Gender and mode of near-death

|       | Mode of death | No. | % |
|-------|---------------|-----|---|
| Men   | Illness       | 10  | 24 |
|       | Accident      | 4   | 10 |
|       | Suicide       | 2   | 5 |
| Women | Illness       | 19  | 46 |
|       | Accident      | 5   | 12 |
|       | Suicide       | 1   | 2 |
|       | Total         | 41  | 100 |

## Non-experiencers

Only three of the respondents I interviewed who formed part of my original sample had been in a life threatening situation where no near-death type experiences were reported. In these cases the patients concerned were receiving heavy doses of medication, which is thought by some to have interfered with the NDE process or its recollection. Since that time I have encountered a number of others who fit into this category, but the amount of cases is not substantial. Such a small percentage of non-experiencers cannot resolve this issue and more research is clearly needed.

Another factor that may have decreased the number of non-experiencers that were forthcoming was the fact that all the American NDErs I interviewed were chosen from the files of people who were known to have had an NDE prior to my meeting with them. In the case of my British respondents, the referrals from various sources nearly all turned out to have had an NDE at the time of their life-threatening episode.

## Some demographic data

Of the total of forty-one people whose cases were examined during the eighteen month research period, thirty-four of these recounted an experience that was predominantly positive, and four reported experiences that were decidedly negative in quality. The remaining three reported that nothing unusual had occurred to them at the time of their near-death episode. In Table 4 are some basic details.

TABLE 4
Demographic information of near-death experiences

| Total interviewed | | No. | % |
|---|---|---|---|
| Sex | Male | 16 | 39 |
| | Female | 25 | 61 |
| Race | Caucasian | 38 | 93 |
| | Other | 3 | 7 |
| Marital Status | Married | 26 | 63 |
| | Single | 7 | 17 |
| | Divorced | 4 | 10 |
| | Widowed | 4 | 10 |

*Conditions of near-death episode*

In concluding this summary of the characteristic features most commonly associated with the NDE, we are left with a final question, namely: Does it make a difference how a person nearly dies? Like the American researchers, I too found evidence to suggest that the circumstances of a person's death make no difference to the likelihood of their having an NDE. Elements of the experience were found in all the three categories that I examined.

It also transpired from the British accounts that people in this country whose near-death episode resulted from illness were both more likely to have an experience, and that they generally tended to reach a deeper level, than the other categories. The Connecticut researchers found that 'accident victims appeared somewhat more likely to experience the life review phenomenon than did respondents in the other two conditions, though this effect was not a strong one statistically'. They originally found that 'suicide victims were never found to have had experiences beyond Stage III, and the experiences they did report tended to depart somewhat from the prototypical pattern'; but subsequent research has indicated that 'NDEs following suicide attempts, however induced, conform to the classic prototype'. In general terms, therefore, all the evidence for reaching the moment of death itself would point to the fact that the process of dying seems to be much the same for almost everyone regardless of how the event is brought about. But, of course, all the people whose near-death episodes have been recounted here came back from the brink of death, so what kind of effects can we expect to find occurring in the lives of those individuals as a result of their having been involved in this incident? What impact has the fact of being so close to one's demise had on them? Does an NDE have the profound effect on the life-style and attitude to others that has been reported in the American studies? In Part Two of this book I will show some of the different ways this experience has influenced the people who returned from death.

# PART TWO

## *Beyond near-death*

# CHAPTER 7
# *After-effects of the near-death experience*

> Experience is not what happens to a man. It is what a man does with what happens to him.
>
> *Aldous Huxley*

As the narratives of the near-death encounters presented in the first part of this book have shown, the experience is so remarkable and so unusual that the passing years do little to obscure the clarity of the memory. And, while many respondents stress that they have never again been able to reach the depth of feeling that the incident imparted, they were nevertheless at pains to emphasise that they are still vividly able to recall the occurrence and that it continues to exert a powerful and singular influence in their lives.

So what is this influence and how does it affect the person who has had an NDE? One of the main themes of my research was to look at the kind of after-effects that one might expect to find as a result of having had this unique experience, and it is this aspect of the near-death encounter that will be the main focus of the second part of this book.

The number of non-experiences in my sample was too small for definite conclusions to be drawn. But for what it is worth, they did feel that their lives had been affected in a way that they were not clearly able to specify, a reaction borne out by the American studies. In contrast, those respondents who had undergone an NDE stated that they felt the experience had made a profound impact on their lives. So it seems that whatever interpretation one chooses to put on the near-death phenomenon, the after-effects are undoubtedly real, and it is this feature that I will be concerned with looking at in the ensuing chapter.

## LIFE CHANGES

One of the most frequently mentioned results of the NDE is a deeply felt shift towards experiencing life in a more positive way, especially with regard to people and nature. These transformations in attitude, which have been likened to a spiritual rebirth, include a personal sense of renewal and a search for purpose and meaning (usually accompanied by personality and value changes with enhanced self-esteem). Many of these people felt that the near-death episode had definitely altered their relationships with others; they found that they became more compassionate and tolerant, and that this change of heart was extended to strangers as well as family and friends. The sense of being reborn, the renewed sense of individual purpose, the determination to live life to its fullest, all reflect the deep and profound changes that the experience engenders. The things that come to have value from henceforward are love and service towards others; material considerations are no longer so important. What becomes significant now is to live life in accordance with this new-found understanding of what really matters.

The most commonly expressed awareness of changes in attitude seem to fall into three main categories; these can be summarised as an enhanced ability to be more open and loving towards others, a desire to attain to more knowledge (described as a thirst for understanding the 'laws of the universe', an understanding quite separate from the accumulation of intellectual information), and an urge to develop inherent gifts and talents to be used for the benefit of others.

### *Love*

The first of these outstanding characteristics is a heightened sense of love and humanity. These are clearly discernible in the two quotes given below, which both come from British respondents.

A woman who nearly died during an operation for the removal of fibroids in her womb put it this way: 'I find it easier to open my heart to people since the experience.' While another woman who was very badly burnt as a result of an accident when her dress caught fire said: 'I find that I am only truly happy when I am doing things for others.' And to give an idea of the similarity of effect that is experienced by both the cultural groups studied, the next two excerpts, which come from the American respondents, clearly show the correspondences.

One of the cardiac victims said something very similar to what has just been quoted when he commented: 'I have such a feeling of love for humanity, for everybody, it radiates out of me, a love like I have never before experienced. I had no idea this had ever happened to anyone else.' A woman who was also the victim of a cardiac arrest acknowledged:

> The things that I felt slowly were a very heightened sense of love, the ability to communicate love, the ability to find joy and pleasure in the smallest and most insignificant things about me. I seemed to develop very strong abilities to be able to communicate with other people. I seemed to have a very heightened awareness, I would say almost telepathic abilities. I developed a great compassion for people that were ill and facing death and I wanted so much to let them know, to somehow make them aware that the dying process was nothing more than an extension of one's life.

A man whose NDE occurred when he was suffering from pneumonia said that since his recovery:

> I think I'm still working on what happened, but I just know I have to be a different kind of person; my view of other people has changed. I have always been a very closed and private person, but this experience has made me open up quite a bit. I feel more loving and more involved with people.

For a number of respondents this enhanced feeling of love was extended towards the world of nature as well as to people. A heightened appreciation of all creation was beautifully expressed by a Jewish man after his NDE, which followed a heart attack:

> Since then, everything has been so different. I go out into the sunlight and I can taste the air; the sky is so blue and the trees are much greener; everything is so much more beautiful. My senses are so much sharper. I can even see auras round trees.

## Knowledge

Among the changes of attitude noted by near-death survivors, those directed towards acquiring an understanding of the established order of things within the cosmos, especially those things that have to do with life and death, are rated as having priority in their newly-developed life-style.

One of the women who nearly died giving birth supplied the following example: 'Since the experience I have been driven by a desire to find out who I am and what I am here for and I need to share this experience with others.' And a respondent who has just given an illustration in the previous section continued his evaluation by saying:

> I had some slight knowledge of the work of Kübler-Ross, but I had never before read or heard anything about this type of experience. I now want to know about this and, although I am not one to read books, I want to try to undestand what has happened to me and aim to do some reading in the future. I would also like to change my life-style and work to help people with these kinds of problems.

Another woman who nearly died giving birth admitted that: 'After my experience I became very interested in psychic phenomena and would try to read books in order to find out more about it. I have always been quite interested in these subjects but became more so after.'

A man who was dying of leukaemia prior to his NDE subsequently assisted the hospital chaplain by recording his experience for a seminar on death and dying that the minister was giving. When asked about his prior knowledge of the phe-nomenon he said:

> He [the chaplain] asked me if I had ever read *Life After Life*, and I told him I had not. But my son got hold of a copy and he brought it over to the house and these people's experiences are very similar to the one I had.

The woman who had been badly burnt concluded her narrative by saying: 'Since that time I have been on a search for the truth and feel that I have some part to play in helping others to discover knowledge which will help humanity.'

The next illustration comes from another woman who nearly died giving birth:

> I feel my life has completely changed as a result of my experience. Although I read *Life After Life* long after my experience, I feel that since that time I have been searching for the real meaning of life and death.

Finally, one of the women who had a negative experience told me that:'As a result of this experience I have become interested in and made a study of comparative religion in my search for the truth.'

## Gifts and talents

Another personality and value change that occurs has to do with the development of inherent gifts and talents that have lain dormant and neglected. The advent of the NDE somehow awakens an awareness that these abilities have been given to us for a purpose and are to be developed and used in the service of humanity. There is never any sense of personal aggrandisement in these inclinations, in fact many people stress the need for personal sacrifice and dedication that is needed in order to fulfil what they see as a divinely inspired mission.

The following statement is typical of the kind of sentiment that is often expressed in this connection. A man whose operation for a double strangulated hernia was complicated by his being haemophiliac said:

> After this incident I began to give thought and recognised that I had the gift of healing. I have now been a practising healer for many years, with the wonderful inner joy of having helped thousands. I am still doing so each week at my home and a healing centre I hold in Birmingham. The sum total is that from the hospital incident I have been reborn. I went through hell to seemingly prepare for this work. My character and thinking etc. drastically changed and I am certainly not the man I was, thank God. Could it be that one is given 'borrowed time' to kind of make amends for one's

unhealthy or unspiritual earlier life? Was the physical and materialistic experience a form of purification or preparation?

A feeling of being reborn was stated by a woman who nearly died of a high fever:

> I felt as if I had emerged from darkness into light. I felt reborn. I know that I am here for a purpose, which is part of God's plan. I feel I am here to learn God's law and to love unconditionally. Since my experience I am no longer content to live life for myself. My sense of fulfilment comes from developing my potential for the benefit of service to others and in this way I also feel I serve God. Material possessions are no longer important. The real riches lie within.

And the man who 'died' for two hours, whose NDE has previously been recounted, found that afterwards:

> All I know is that it's made all the difference to my life. It's given me a purpose and a joy. A determination to help other people. I know I was sent back because I've got work to do for God. I now know that there are laws governing the universe. God does not break these laws, they are part of his own nature. But when we transgress these laws, suffering and disease follow and the only way to reverse this is to learn to live in harmony with God's laws.

As the sentiments just expressed have shown, a number of NDErs find that they spontaneously develop the ability to heal. Others find that they have become clairvoyant following their near-death episode. Still others discover inherent gifts and abilities seen as manifestations of God within, which their encounter with the light or source of all life and creativity somehow activated so as to enable them to develop and use these qualities for the benefit of themselves and others. The fear of ridicule and disbelief that encourages suppression of the results of this experience must be countered in order that these after-effects can be allowed expression, not only for the benefit of the individual concerned, but also for the advantage of the whole human family. These subsequent realisations, which contain an awareness that life is a sacred gift, are coupled with a desire to understand the 'real' meaning of life's mysteries and a firm resolve to live life to its fullest. Other after-effects include a sense of rebirth and renewal, a renewed sense of purpose, a new-found inner strength and an increased self-confidence, together with unconditional love and a sense of service to mankind.

Table 5 represents a summary of the reported changes that have a bearing on the transformative aspects involved in the NDE. These figures are based on responses to specific questions I asked towards the end of my interviews with the experiencers. In a few cases where these questions were not asked, the individual was coded as unchanged for each item.

TABLE 5
Life changes resulting from the near-death experience

|  | No. changed | % | No. unchanged | % |
|---|---|---|---|---|
| More positive attitude to life | 24 | 59 | 17 | 41 |
| Life lived more fully | 19 | 46 | 22 | 54 |
| Sense of rebirth | 14 | 34 | 27 | 66 |
| Renewed sense of purpose and meaning | 22 | 54 | 19 | 46 |
| Enhanced sense of self-worth | 16 | 39 | 25 | 61 |
| More personal power | 20 | 49 | 21 | 51 |
| More disinterested | 12 | 29 | 29 | 71 |
| More loving and compassionate | 23 | 56 | 18 | 44 |
| Less attached to material possessions | 13 | 32 | 28 | 68 |
| Fewer expectations | 12 | 29 | 29 | 71 |
| Greater empathy | 21 | 51 | 20 | 49 |
| Greater understanding and discrimination | 15 | 37 | 26 | 63 |

## CONCEPTUAL CHANGES

One of the most significant effects of the NDE is that it tends to diminish the fear of death. Both positive and negative experiences inclined the participant to the view that life continues after death. This includes not only a belief in heaven and hell, but also a belief in God, or some supreme power for good, as well as a conviction that some force for evil also exists.

## Changes in attitude towards death

The distinctive attitudes of this change of view in regard to what happens after death are well illustrated in the following comments. I will start with a number of observations made by British NDErs in connection with this aspect and then, as on previous occasions, move on to show the similarity of attitude expressed by the American respondents.

The woman who had an NDE as a result of being very badly burnt observed: 'I do not fear death anymore as I now know that there is a wonderful life after death.' While the woman who nearly died from a kidney infection put it this way:

I have lost all fear of death, I almost welcome it, but at the same time I would never do anything to precipitate it. I feel we are here for a purpose and we cannot avoid what we have come here for.

The young girl who was clinically dead for twenty minutes when she contracted a brain virus remarked: 'I am not afraid of dying. I know that there's something better because I'm convinced I've been there.' The woman who was seriously ill with a virus infection during which time she had an NDE felt: 'I'm no longer afraid of death, for since my experience I know there is so much to look forward to.' A woman who nearly died following a road accident said afterwards: 'If this is a near-death experience then I no longer have any fear of dying as it is such a beautiful occurrence.'

It will by now have become apparent from these comments that one of the strongest subjective impressions that I gained throughout the course of discussing their NDEs with the respondents is that loss of, or a greatly decreased, fear of death is one of the main points of difference between them and the non-experiencers. While it is tempting to go on giving more excerpts in order to convey just how frequently these observations are made with regard to this change of attitude, I feel the point has already been amply made with the comments that have been related thus far; so I will conclude these examples with just two more from my British sample quotes before moving on to look at the comparative illustrations.

A similar opinion to the ones just related was supplied by one of the women whose NDE occurred during a very difficult labour: 'Since my experience I no longer have any fear of death as I now know for sure that there is life after death. My only fear is of the physical process leading up to death.' Lastly, one of the heart attack victims had this to say about his near-death episode:

> I felt in awe of the experience, but I have never been frightened of the idea of dying since then. Before the experience I always thought death was the end, that there was nothing more. It had a very profound effect on me.

In the following reports, which came from the American respondents, it is evident that the same powerful influence is exerted on those people who have had an NDE, providing a potent antidote to the fear associated with dying. Also, this effect, this feeling of confidence, is not just experienced at the moment of death, but continues to be effective throughout the remainder of the recipient's life. While the number of non-experiencers in my original sample was too small to allow me to come to any valid conclusions with regard to this or any other aspect of NDE comparison, I have since then spoken to many more people in this category and found that no such systematic change is experienced, certainly not the emphatic and sometimes emotionally charged statements that have come to be associated with NDErs when reporting these effects. Furthermore, this consequence has been noted in the American studies which emphasise that it is the fact of having a 'core experience' that appears to be crucial in this regard and not the fact of having come close to death *per se*.

I will start the comparative accounts by quoting an example which comes from the man whose NDE resulted from a ruptured ulcer. He observed:

> To go through the pain and all, up to that point, well I don't think I could go through it again, but at the end it was so beautiful that I am not afraid of it. . . . All I know is that I was there, I'm not afraid of it and that it's something beautiful . . . I don't fear death any more. I still fear the physical pain that can precede death, but death itself I fear no more.

One of the respondents who was the victim of a heart attack commented: 'It was, I believe, is, I believe, a moment of transition from one state of consciousness to a very high and intensely beautiful state of consciousness.' From the man whose NDE was caused by blood in his lungs due to pneumonia: 'I have never had any real fear of death, but now I feel it is something to look forward to.' And the man who 'died' from the results of a haemorrhage said: 'Life is but a moment; there is no death, only transition.' The man who had a very deep NDE when he was crushed under a truck also acknowledged:

> As a result of this experience I have no fear of death. If a life-threatening situation came about I would certainly do everything I could to avoid it, but I know that when my time comes I want to consciously relax and let this come about. If death is anything like what I experienced, it has to be the most wonderful thing to look forward to.

The last comment on the change of feeling with regard to dying and death comes from the transcript of a woman whose experience was reported in the Connecticut study. Her case history, which I obtained from the archives of IANDS, was chosen to be included among my American respondents as in Kenneth Ring's view she gave 'the strongest opinion concerning loss of fear' in this connection. Her NDE occurred as a result of a heart attack. Afterwards she remarked:

> I was always afraid of death. Well, I faced death those three weeks that I was in the hospital. They never knew whether my heart would stop or not. . . . I had absolutely no fear at all. The first time in my life that I was actually face to face with death and I wasn't afraid. . . . Since then I have had another heart attack and I was not afraid at all. In fact everyone was amazed. I face death every day now . . . and I know I could die at any time, but I'm not afraid of it . . . . In all this critical time I was not afraid. I'm not afraid as I know what death is. It's not the end but the beginning. Life is a gift from God, I would never give it up. I would always hang on to it. But I'm not afraid of it. I know there's something up there for me.

From all that has been quoted it can easily be seen that the effect of having an NDE makes a great difference to one's concept of death. Both sets of respondents commented that their fear of death was diminished by their changed understanding of what happens when death occurs, but qualified their comments by saying that they nevertheless still feared the physical pain that can sometimes occur prior to death. In both groups respondents mentioned looking forward to death, but said that life was a gift not to be given up. As these observations have shown, not only is the NDE strikingly similar in both the cross-cultural groups studied, but the after-effects show a marked similarity as well.

### Belief in life after death

A related question concerned the changes in belief as to whether life continues after death. Along with the other questions that dealt with possible post-incident convictions, this topic was brought up after the respondent had given a free narrative of the NDE events. In many cases this information was volunteered during the course of the report, but I usually followed up the history of the incident by asking a number of specific questions that touched upon the after-effects directly. The results of this inquiry can be seen in the ensuing accounts.

A woman who collapsed and 'died' while she was being rushed to hospital by ambulance later stated: 'What happened to me at that time is the most unusual experience I've ever had. It has made me realise that there is life after death.' A man who 'died' several times during a heart attack before his condition became stable asserted: 'I used not to believe in life after death, but now I've changed my mind.' And the woman who had a kidney infection added this to her former statement: 'I also know that there is a real life to which we go, which is so much more than the existence which we have here.' The woman who nearly died as a result of major abdominal surgery declared: 'I always felt we continued after death, but this has given me a certainty that life goes on.'

As these excerpts reveal, people who have had an NDE are significantly more likely to believe in a life that continues after death than those who have not. Furthermore, as was the case with their attitude towards death, it is the fact of their having been through the stages enumerated by Dr Ring that made the difference to their conviction of a life hereafter, and not the actuality of coming close to death as such. These changes in attitude, then, and the consequent decrease in the fear of death, are brought about by the changes in concept that result from having a 'core experience'; which brings us to the next consideration, namely, what effect does the NDE have on the participants' attitude to God?

## Changes in relationship to God

With the exception of two respondents who did not have any faith in God or belief in an after life prior to their NDE, most of the respondents felt that it was the increased certainty that God exists, and the subsequent intensity of their feeling for Him, that had changed as a result of their NDE. To those respondents who had experienced being in the presence of a Being of overwhelming light and love, which many understood to be God or Jesus, the tendency to relate to Him in a much more personal way, and with far greater depth of emotion than previously, was a natural outcome.

A woman who was very badly burnt as a result of an accident responded to my questions about the possible effect her experience might have had on her belief in God with the following comment: 'I believe in God and Jesus more firmly than ever, but my concept of them has changed.' Another woman who was brought up as an Anglican Catholic said that after her NDE: 'I know I have a close connection with someone who is always there for me, but I do not believe in God as taught by religion any more. I also now believe that we come back again.' The increased depth of feeling just referred to was expressed by the woman who nearly died due to a kidney infection. She said in answer to my inquiry regarding this issue:

> My experience has not changed my beliefs, but rather enhanced them. I now have an absolute certainty that God, call him what you will, 'the big silver bird that comes out of the sky', exists in a very real way.

The woman who came very near to death when her temperature reached 105° during a virus infection found:

> Since that time I feel much closer to God and can sense his presence whenever I draw close to Him. I also find that

many of my prayers are answered in a most miraculous way and I get answers to many of the problems that I am confronted with when I ask for guidance.

Lastly, to end these comments on the changes in attitude towards death, life after death and relationship to God, I am including a quote from another accident victim who was badly injured in a car crash. She summed up all three conceptual changes when she said: 'Since then my belief in God has increased and also my belief in life after death. I also have less fear of death.'

The overall feeling that was transmitted during the process of assessing these conceptual changes was that the NDE had definitely brought about a heightened spiritual awareness in those people who had undergone it. This involved a sense of being closer to God and communicating with Him at a very personal level, but generally being less interested in formal religious involvement. An endorsement of non-sectarian attitudes was combined with feelings that all religions are basically the same. In Table 6 these changes of feeling with regard to death and life after death, along with changes in conception of God experienced by respondents following their NDE, are summed up.

TABLE 6
Changes in attitude to death, life after death and God.

|                                        | No. changed | % | No. unchanged | % |
|----------------------------------------|-------------|-----|---------------|-----|
| Decrease in fear of death              | 26          | 63  | 15            | 37  |
| Increase in belief of life after death | 31          | 76  | 10            | 24  |
| Concept of heaven                      | 14          | 34  | 27            | 66  |
| Concept of hell                        | 23          | 56  | 18            | 44  |
| Belief in God                          | 11          | 27  | 30            | 73  |
| Concept of God                         | 15          | 37  | 26            | 63  |

## Changes in religious attitudes

Concurrent with an altered attitude towards death, life after death and God, there is a changed perception with regard to religion. Although most of the respondents came from orthodox religious background, the majority underwent a significant change in their concept of death and their expectations of an afterlife as a result of their experience. The individual's prior religious attitude does not appear to affect the likelihood of an NDE occurring, but the experience undoubtedly changes the person's relationship to religion subsequently. The main shift would seem to be away from theological doctrines to a more spiritual ideology. They tend to be less dependent on the religious interpretations of the church, and more contemplative and private in their beliefs. Typical examples of the difference in feeling towards religion that is likely to be encountered in people after an NDE are given below. They convey something of the characteristic changes just mentioned.

A woman who had an NDE while undergoing an operation for the removal of her womb had this to say:'Although I am still a Roman Catholic, I feel the experience I had is beyond any denomination.' A similar stance was taken by one of the women who came very close to death as a result of having a very difficult time giving birth. She took her revised perspective even further when she said:

> I was raised in the Church of England, but since my experience I have become non-denominational. I now feel all religion is basically the same and I think there should be a world religion which would put an end to the religious divisions and the problems that this causes.

Another woman who was also brought up as an Anglican, but who subsequently changed her religious affiliation to that of spiritualism after having an NDE following a serious car accident, told me:

> Afterwards I wanted to develop my spiritual awareness and to learn the true meaning of the cosmos and my own relationship with God. I was no longer content just to take on face value what I was told by a priest. I feel I don't have to go to any particular church to find God. Whether it's a Protestant Church or a synagogue, it's all the same to me.

I found that quite a number of respondents either became non-denominational or turned to theosophical or psychical associations after their NDE, as they felt that their former religious affiliations were unable to provide answers to the questions that they were so ardently seeking to understand. The philosophical doctrines proposed by these organisations seemed to be more in accord with their own changed perspectives.

The next remark to be made in this connection came from the woman who had a cardiac arrest while under the anaesthetic having a tooth extracted. She was also formerly Church of England, but became a member of the Spiritualist Association of Great Britain after her NDE. What she said concerning her feelings with regard to this is as follows: 'I don't belong to any particular church any more. I am equally at home in any church. Any religion is basically saying the same thing. It's human beings that cause divisions.' And the woman who nearly died of a high fever while suffering from a virus infection said:

> I could never make any sense of the things I was taught in church about the bible sayings and the things I was expected to believe about heaven and hell. But since my experience I find I am able to go within for the anwers and suddenly everything makes sense.

The American man who was crushed under a truck provides us with the final comment on this aspect of changed conceptual attitudes, and shows once again the similarity of feeling that the NDE engenders regardless of any cultural differences:

> I am a Catholic and have participated faithfully in my religion, but since reaching maturity I have had my doubts about the dogma. I started to study and to try to understand the basics of other religions. I feel a faith in God gives purpose and meaning to human life, but I could not go along with the way I saw many people practising their religion. Since my experience I have had many questions concerning religion answered.

On the whole, the accounts disclosed that while there was an increased inclination towards being more religious in the true sense of the word, there was a proportionately marked aversion to any kind of bigotry that often attaches to different sects. Rather, the changes took the form of an awakened sense of a higher controlling power and the ability to be able to communicate with this supreme being at any time by going within oneself.

The impression that emerges from this inquiry into the changes

of attitude that concern some of life's perennial issues is that it is
the NDE, as previously noted, that triggers this transformation.
These changes include an increased sense of God within, the loss
of interest in outward religious forms, a spirit of religious
tolerance and a newly-sensed cosmic spirituality. All these
combine towards a renewal of attitude that focuses on the
importance of unconditional love and true spiritual values. It
should be noted, however, that while a spiritual awakening is
more often the case than not, it is not necessarily inevitable, as the
number of respondents who reported no change in their religious
views, while small, reveals. Those who had a hell-like experience
generally felt it was a warning for them to change their way of life
and attitude towards others. That they had been given another
chance to do this led to much 'soul searching' and was often
followed by a change in perception leading on to a different
approach to other people as well as to religious doctrine.

Respondents were asked a number of questions at the end of the
interview designed to elicit information about their religious
beliefs prior to and following their near-death episode. The results
of these changes are presented in Table 7.

TABLE 7
Religious changes arising from the near-death experience

| Religious changes | Protestant | Catholic | Other | None | Total | % |
|---|---|---|---|---|---|---|
| More intense religious feelings | 7 | 9 | 2 | 0 | 18 | 44 |
| Change to alternative beliefs | 11 | 0 | 0 | 0 | 11 | 27 |
| Non-denominational philosophies | 3 | 2 | 1 | 2 | 8 | 20 |
| No change | 2 | 0 | 2 | 0 | 4 | 10 |
| Total no. | 23 | 11 | 5 | 2 | 41 | 100 |
| % | 56 | 27 | 12 | 5 | 100 | |

## *Belief in heaven and hell*

There is one more question that requires our attention before concluding this chapter on the after-effects of the NDE, and that is the views respondents have concerning their beliefs in heaven and hell. On the whole I found that the experience did not tend to change the views people held prior to their NDE, it was more the intensity of their feelings with regard to their beliefs that showed a marked difference. Beliefs in heaven were generally more common than those of hell, but it appeared that NDErs were significantly more likely to undergo a change in their feelings about these issues than non-experiencers. To complete this survey, I will end with a few representative quotes that demonstrate this attitude.

The woman who suffered from heart disease gave this very terse answer in reply to my question regarding her belief in heaven: 'Of course I believe in heaven because I've been there.' From the woman who had a virus infection came this response: 'Before my experience I always hoped that heaven existed, but I was never really sure. Now I know that there really is a heaven because I have been there and that makes all the difference.' The man who had an NDE during a heart attack said in reply to this inquiry: 'I have always believed in heaven, but now I'm even more sure as there is absolutely no doubt in my mind that the place I went to was heaven.' While the woman who found herself on the verge of the pit of hell during a negative experience said: 'Before this happened I never believed in hell. I felt God would never create such a place. But since then I have realised that there not only is such a place, but that both good and evil exist.' This view was not shared by everyone, however, for as one respondent who had a deep 'core experience' put it: 'I feel that there is no hell that we "go to". Hell is here. The early Christians saw no separation of heaven and hell.'

To sum up the after-effects of the NDE, most of the research that has been carried out to date tends to suggest that the experience is profoundly transforming, particularly with regard to the greatly reduced fear of death that results. My own research generally supports the assertion that many of those who survive a near-death episode do indeed change in a significant way.

That the episode represents for many an experience that is

definitely spiritual in its overtones is beyond question. For most, the subjective quality of exceptional 'realness' is taken to mean, quite unequivocally, that there is life after death. This needs to be recognised when evaluating the transformational nature of the experience. The fact of surviving a near-death episode is seen as having been given another chance to live life anew, and this is expressed by living it more fully, lovingly and meaningfully. It is hardly surprising, therefore, in view of the extremely vivid and subjectively authentic manner in which the impressions of their experience are transmitted, that their life should now seem more grounded in a sense of purpose and more consciously shaped by the spiritual values of love, compassion and acceptance. In view of the fact that the implications of the NDE are regarded as real by those who have experienced them, it would seem only reasonable to expect that changes of this nature would occur.

While the experience is reported as being so striking and singular that the passage of time does nothing to dim its vividness, it rarely remains merely a memory as such, but rather seems to be a continuing active force that seeks to promote growth in life-affirming ways that exert a powerful influence on an individual's motivations, values and conduct. Thus, the results of this investigation into the after-effects of NDEs would seem to bear out the evidence of the American studies and together they produce a fairly clear image of this aspect of near-death phenomena.

# CHAPTER 8
# *Paranormal developments following near-death experiences*

Men's minds perceive second causes,
But only prophets perceive the action of the First Cause.

*Jalal-uddin-Rumi*

Recently there has been a movement among a large section of the population on either side of the Atlantic towards a feeling that many, if not all, of the ultimate secrets of the universe will only be revealed through unusual and so far largely unexplored areas of inquiry. This impetus has led to a powerful spiritual challenge to traditional religious faith and a resurgence of many unorthodox ways of attempting to contact the source of universal knowledge, which in former and more repressive times would have been attended by very severe penalties.

It has long been known that many of the early Christian heretics, such as the Cathars, were possessed of gifts that nowadays would come under the heading of paranormal. Today these concepts are attracting the attention and imagination of people on an ever-increasing scale, and for many of those who become involved an allegiance to their chosen group is developed that far exceeds any previous sense of commitment they felt for the old order. The main difference between the mass of people who are turning away from orthodox religion in search of something that has a more personal meaning, and the people who have had a near-death episode, is that it is almost always the NDE that precipitates the change in their case.

One of the consequences of the NDE is that it often has the effect of making available to the recipient certain inexplicable talents, such as those of apparent extra-sensory perception and

113

healing, which the individual was often not aware of possessing prior to his or her near-death event. The number of respondents who have developed these gifts quite spontaneously as a result of their NDE, while small, forms one of the most provocative sub-groups to be studied and it is this phenomenon that will next be the focus of our attention.

In cases where these perceptions appear to take place within the context of the life review phase of the NDE, Kenneth Ring has suggested that these instances should perhaps be construed as possible 'life previews', in order to distinguish them from past events. In other instances, the perceptions that are reported seem to relate not so much to the personal future of the individual as to global incidents, and in these instances Dr Ring recommends that they are best understood as 'world events'. In order to differentiate them he has coined the terms 'personal flashfor-wards' (PFFs) for those cases which contain individual information and 'prophetic visions' (PVs) for those which relate to universal circumstances.

Obviously, it is most important to attempt to arrive at an assessment of the portent of these prophesies in order to increase the understanding of NDEs in general. But there is another issue which captures the imagination, and it is that if these precognitive visions are correct, by endeavouring to determine their possible accuracy, not only will they be of great interest to many as they deal with coming world events, but they will also serve to bear out the prophetic claims that have already been made regarding these events by seers as far apart as Nostradamus and Edgar Cayce.

Because Kenneth Ring is the only researcher to have carried out a study of this aspect of NDEs, as far as I am aware, I will be making substantial reference to his findings which were first reported in *Anabiosis: The Journal for Near-Death Studies*. He points out that as the number of cases in his sample was small, based on approximately thirteen examples, it was not possible to undertake any meaningful statistical analysis, and that the results would have to be independently validated before they could be fully accepted. Nevertheless he felt justified in publishing his data in view of the potential significance of his findings.

## EXTRA-SENSORY PERCEPTION

The ability to have access to knowledge not usually present to the senses is one of the elements associated with having an NDE. This seems to happen in one of two ways. In the first, information concerning coming events is given during a life review and is seen within the context of one's life assessment, which is typically described as an image or vision of the future. In this case an individual will become aware of having knowledge of future events after recovery from an NDE. These are the cases that would come within the category of a life preview. In the second, this ability seems to develop as a direct result of having had an NDE, so it appears that it is the incident itself which is responsible for triggering some mechanism whereby this becomes possible following the event. In these instances they are probably best perceived as coming within the realm of extra-sensory perception. I will start my examination of these paranormal developments by first reviewing this aspect.

### Telepathy and precognition

The phenomenon which we are concerned with here includes two distinct types of ESP. In the first, there is telepathy, which involves communication between two beings at a distance without external means. In the second, we are dealing with prediction, which usually foretells of events that are likely to happen and which extend beyond the range of 'chance variation'. Respondents generally claim that these powers developed as a direct result of their NDE, and that for the most part they were not aware that there was any evidence for their having abilities of this kind prior to their near-death encounter.

A woman respondent whom I saw shortly after she had been discharged from Charing Cross Hospital, following an attack of hyperventilation during which time she had an out-of-the-body experience while she was unconscious, told me:

> Since this experience I have noticed that I seem to have become clairvoyant, as I find it is possible to be in telepathic rapport with people. This has happened to me a number of

times recently, as I find that when I am thinking about a
friend whom I met in the hospital who had a similar
experience to me and I am about to telephone her, at that
same moment the phone rings and it is her on the line. This
has happened on two or three occasions since the experience
and I never had anything like that happen to me before.

I was able to confirm this statement subsequently when I talked
with the friend in question who assured me that this was indeed
the case.

And from another woman I saw in Charing Cross Hospital who
was also suffering from the same syndrome: 'When I am feeling
very low and exhausted I get sightings or pictures of events that
are going to happen, which later come true. So now I take this as a
warning when it happens.' While the woman whose NDE
happened as a result of an operation to remove her womb said: 'I
can't explan how, but I am clairvoyant now, which developed
since then.' A woman whose NDE resulted from a major
abdominal operation, and who has not been referred to before,
reported:

> Afterwards I found I was able to see future events. When this
> happens I feel as if I am taken over by a power or force
> greater than myself. At the time of my experience I was told
> that in the future things would be very difficult, but also
> quite sternly that this was necessary.

In the cases just related it is obvious that all the respondents felt
that they had become clairvoyant since their NDE, and as a result
were either able to sense impending events or were able to see
pictures of future incidents, and while they are all quite explicit on
this point there is still only the suggestion of paranormal
knowledge and not any specific accounts of the portent so far.
Later, I will be looking at the content of these perceptions, but
before doing so I want to consider another category of
paranormal development which deals with the discernment of
coming events. On these occasions automatic writing is the
medium through which the information is disclosed.

## Automatic writing

Another related phenomenon which seems to parallel the process of receiving clairvoyant information, either through messages heard or pictures seen, which concerns both 'personal flashfor-wards' and prophetic visions, is the development of automatic writing which can also occur as a consequence of having had an NDE. As in the cases of ESP, respondents usually aver that this ability did not exist prior to their experience. The next two quotes illustrate this assertion.

The man who was on the point of committing suicide by taking an overdose of mandrax tablets when he had an NDE told me:

> I was directed to pick up a pencil and a piece of paper and as I started to write I felt as if someone was writing through me, as if I was taken over by a higher source. I was given answers to many of the problems of life and understood many things that were due to happen. I had never been able to do this before my experience.

And the woman whose NDE happened when she nearly died from a virus infection in the spinal cord said: 'I have a document case which is now crammed full of "Automatic writing" which commenced also at that time and has continued regularly ever since.'

If these apparent communications are authentic, it can be readily understood that they would be likely to exert a very powerful influence on the individual, especially if and when the predictions were later confirmed. In the next category I will be concerned with looking at the precognitive phenomenon that is usually reported in association with the life review, and which generally occurs during the deeper NDEs, in order to see whether the information obtained at that time endorses the events that are encountered subsequently.

## Life preview

During the life preview the events are experienced within the same timeless framework that has been described elsewhere, so that past, present and future all seem to be happening at once. As Kenneth Ring has put it: 'It is as though the individual sees something of the whole trajectory of his life, not just past events as some previous accounts (e.g. Moody, 1975; Noyes, 1977) have implied.' While the events seen appear to represent circumstances that will probably happen, these events are nevertheless conditional on the choice to return to life, so that to the near-death survivor it will be like a 'memory' of future events. This is understood in the context of an intended design (previously mentioned) which occurs in connection with the decision to return phase of the NDE.

The few examples that are included here give an idea of the impressions that are gained during a life preview. The first comes from the woman who had a virus infection. She had this to say:

> At this time I was shown the pattern of my entire life and I was made to understand that everything that happens, even the bad times, happen in order to teach one certain lessons, and that these are not to punish one, but to teach one certain lessons that are necessary for one's spiritual development.

A similar message was given to the woman whose NDE resulted from heart failure during an abdominal operation; she recalled:

> I was told at the time of my NDE that the difficult circumstances that I was going through at that time were happening in order to teach me certain lessons, but that by a certain age all the obstacles would be removed and that I would be living an entirely different sort of life. All this has come about just as I saw it.

The man who was crushed under a truck said that during his NDE he found that

> The other thing that you realise when you are in the presence of the light is that you are suddenly in communication with absolute knowledge. It's hard to describe, but the nearest I can get to it is that you can think of a question and immediately the answer will come to you. It's as simple as that. It can be on anything whatsoever, even a subject that you don't know anything about. You may not even understand what you receive, but you will instantly be given

the answer and will immediately perceive the meaning. You have only to have an idea of the question and you will immediately receive the correct answer. It's so staggering, I can only compare it to being plugged into a computer and instantly being given the correct answer. I had many questions answered, some of which are extremely personal, some of which have to do with the way a person lives his life and its consequences, some to do with religious questions, as well as certain details on future events.

In other instances the 'flashforward' will only be recalled at the time of the actual event, which seems to have the effect of jogging the individual's memory of it. When this happens it is usually accompanied by an uncanny feeling of *déjà vu*, where awareness of having prior knowledge of an event that is happening and the event itself takes place at the same moment. An example of the kind of impression that this experience evokes is quoted below.

One of the women who almost died during a very prolonged labour while giving birth to her daughter said:

During the experience I was aware that I already knew everything that was going to happen to me. But afterwards I could only recall fragments. I do remember that it was communicated to me that when it was necessary for me to know certain things I could be able to recall them. I have since found this to be the case, as sometimes when things happen I realise I already know how it's going to work out.

Kenneth Ring gives a couple of examples which not only bear out this contention, but also give specific instances of very clear visual impressions of future events that subsequently worked out exactly as had been foreseen. The first concerns a woman who had an NDE as a result of a torn cervix while giving birth. She stated that she learned that there was a time for her to die, but that particular time was not it. She was further told that if she continued down the path she was on at that time (it seems that she had complete freedom of choice) she would later be living HERE and DOING THIS. She said that during the preview she found herself in a place that was not the one she had expected to move to. She then went on to describe a domestic scene in which she saw her children as grown-ups with herself and her husband, who had become middle-aged by then. Many years later she subsequently found herself re-enacting this same scene, in the place that she had foreseen, doing exactly what she had seen happening. What makes this case remarkable is that at the time an exception was made regarding the five physical senses. She found she was not only able to see and hear what was going on during her 'personal flashforward' but that she was also able to smell. She went on to say that:

> Particularly striking was the smell of the salad I was producing [cucumber] mingled with the smell of evergreens growing around the house and the odour of freshly cut grass. Also, I could detect my own cologne and soap from the shower my husband had vacated. This picture was only a glimpse, but it made a huge impression on me. I must have vowed right then never to forget it, because I certainly have not.

The second example he gives, which, as he says, 'exemplifies most of the characteristics of finely detailed PFFs', was sent to him by a correspondent who wrote that as a ten-year-old child while living in England (his native country), he was rushed to hospital and operated on for acute appendicitis. During the operation he had an NDE while out of his body (he was also able to see his body while this was happening), at which time he communicated telepathically with beings who seemed to be clothed in robes. He was conscious that after the operation, while convalescing, he had some strange memories concerning events in his future life, but at the time he simply did not believe them. He goes on to describe five specific 'memories', all of which he claims have actually come about as events in his life, except for the last one which pertains to the age and circumstances of his death. He was made aware that he would be married at age twenty-eight, which did indeed happen, even though, as he points out, 'at my twenty-eighth birthday I had yet to meet the person that I was to marry.' He was also told that he would have two children and live in the house that he was shown. Like the woman in the previous account, he too suddenly realised one day that he was living the 'memory' from his past experience. He further states: 'But it was not seeing the future, in the conventional sense, it was *experiencing* the

future. In this incident the future was *now*.' He points out that it is
*not possible* for a ten-year-old boy to know what it feels like to be
married, but that it was this 'strange and impossible feeling that I
remember so clearly, and why this incident remained in my mind'.
The sequel to this experience is noteworthy as he says that, in the
scene which he saw during his PFF, he was in a room with his wife
and two children and was aware that behind the wall there was
something very strange that he did not understand. He recalls:
'My conscious mind could not grasp it, but I just *knew* that
something different was there.' When he later found himself
reliving what he had already experienced he 'began to realise that
there was something to these strange recollections'. For the
strange object behind the walls turned out to be a forced-air heater
and these heating units were not in use in England at that time. He
concluded: 'That is why I could not grasp what it was; it was not
in my sphere of knowledge in 1941.'

While it is easy to imagine the kind of effect that these
experiences must have on the individual, we are nevertheless
confronted by a difficult problem, namely, how do we know these
accounts are true? While it seems unlikely that all the people
reporting these experiences are fabricating (indeed many claim
that some events foreseen have already taken place), they are
nevertheless both largely unproven and unprovable self-reports.

This leaves us in the awkward position of having to accept that
these experiences can occur, while lacking the means of verifying
much of what is reported. Kenneth Ring has observed that, 'This
of course is a general problem in near-death studies, and it has
compelled at least one investigator (Sabom, 1982) to focus on
potentially confirmable aspects of NDEs in order to avoid it.' All
the same, there are some instances, admittedly rare, when this
problem can be overcome by tracing the external evidence that
corroborates the claims made by respondents. A case in point is
the well-attested account reported by Raymond Moody in his
book *Reflections on Life After Life* (1975) of a woman who
during her NDE was shown a picture of him by her guides and
told that she would meet this man, whose name was Moody,
when the time was right in order to tell him her story.

I now propose to move on to another aspect of the precognitive
phenomena associated with NDEs, one where the precognitions

are more universal in their content. I refer to the prophetic visions of world events that have been reported by a number of respondents on both sides of the Atlantic.

## World events

Concurrent with the life preview just reviewed is another phenomenon that can occur at the same time. This occurrence, which concerns prophetic visions (PVs), differs in a couple of significant respects from PFFs. In the first place they relate to world events and thus have a global rather than personal orientation; and in the second, as will be seen, there is a remarkable degree of similarity between the predictions forecast. It is this correspondence of content, together with the specific events which are related, that makes these PVs a matter of such grave concern (given the possible outcome of their oracular nature).

It seems from the accounts of those respondents who relate a PV that these scenes of world events are generally communicated in one of two ways. Either the PVs occurred during their NDE, in which case respondents often feel that it was their guides or the being of light who allowed them to have a glimpse of these future events, or alternatively these visions of the future manifest after the NDE. In these instances it appears as though knowledge, imprinted at the time of their near-death encounter, gradually becomes evident subsequent to the incident itself. However, what emerges into consciousness on these occasions is evidently only the 'tip of the iceberg', for it seems that much more information lies submerged below the surface waiting to appear when the time is right for the message to be released. In fact, some individuals claim that they were told at the time that they would not be able to recall everything, but would only have access to it when and if the need arose.

The kind of comment that is made with regard to this knowledge and the way in which the information will be made available was given by the respondent whose NDE resulted from complications that developed during a hysterectomy:

Afterwards I knew that I had far more knowledge than I

could recall of future events concerning my own life and the way that coming world events would affect it. . . . They also told me that I would not be able to remember everything, but that as and when it was necessary for me to know I would remember.

A similar statement which also hinted at impending world events was made by the woman who experienced these incidents when she had a very high fever from a virus infection. In this case, however, we are given an indication that these events are not totally unavoidable:

During my experience I became aware of everything that had ever happened and everything that was going to happen – all my past lives and all the future lives I would have. I was also shown events that are likely to happen in the near future, but was made to understand that nothing is absolutely fixed and that everything depends on how we choose to use our own free will, that even those events that are already predestined can be changed or modified by a change in our own way of relating to them.

As I have already intimated, the accounts of the reported PVs are so strikingly similar that, even allowing for the fact that every experience is unique, it is nevertheless possible for an overall picture to be constructed as the elements that comprise these visions are seen to recur over and over again. This fact prompted Kenneth Ring to summarise the events that have been predicted in the following manner, but he qualified this construction by stating that, 'Any overall account must be regarded as *extremely* provisional', and further adds 'It is chiefly the fact that everyone I have talked to has given me a PV that conforms, at least broadly, to this model that emboldens me to offer it at all at this time.'

There is, first of all, a sense of having total knowledge, but specifically one is aware of seeing the entirety of the earth's evolution and history from the beginning to the end of time. The future scenario, however, is usually of short duration, seldom extending much beyond the beginning of the twenty-first century. The individual reports that in this decade there will be an increasing incidence of earthquakes, volcanic activity and generally massive geophysical changes.

There will be resultant disturbances in weather pattern and food supplies. The world economic system will collapse, and the possibility of nuclear war or accident is very great (respondents are not agreed on *whether* a nuclear catastrophe will occur). All of these events are transitional rather than ultimate, however, and they will be followed by a new era in human history, marked by human brother-hood, universal love and world peace. Though many will die, the earth will live. While agreeing that the dates for these events are not fixed, most individuals feel that they are likely to take place during the 1980s.

In order to be able to receive these impressions it would seem that the recipients need to be in a state of consciousness whereby they have access to total knowledge. This condition, from a subjective point of view, is exactly the state that individuals find themselves in during an NDE. It is not as if during the experience they acquire this knowledge, but rather that they become aware at this time that they are already in possession of all knowledge; that they *are* that knowledge.

The events that they are made especially cognisant of at this time, during their panoramic visions, are those that concern the immediate future; for it seems that this is where the greatest urgency currently lies, and it is for this reason that they are permitted either to retain this knowledge in conscious memory after their resuscitation from the near-death state, or to be alerted to conscious awareness of this information afterwards. These visions of world events include a number of very specific incidents which are comprised of geophysical changes, meteorological changes, the breakdown of economic systems, the disruption of vital supplies, social disorder and unrest, and finally nuclear disaster and germ warfare.

The following excerpts will give an idea of the extent of the conditions just referred to, as well as giving an indication of some of the conditions under which this information would seem to re-emerge. I will start by giving a number of examples provided by English illustrations and end each category whenever possible with a quote from the American samples given by Kenneth Ring in his survey of this phenomenon. In this way can be shown the similarity of communication that is reported by both sets of respondents.

## EARTHQUAKES

We will know that the time for the changes that are going to occur has started to happen when there are earthquakes which will take place simultaneously in both the Middle East and Japan.

There are going to be a lot of upheavals such as earthquakes and volcanoes occurring in the next few years, which are going to get increasingly worse. I was given to understand that these activities are a reflection of all the social upheaval and violence that is going on all over the world at the moment.

I saw illegal underground testing going on in the vicinity of faults in the earth's crust, resulting in a series of earthquakes being triggered off around the world. It seemed to me that the people concerned knew of the risks involved, but still went ahead anyway. It was as if they were possessed of some sort of terrible madness which was totally destructive of everyone and everything.

The seismic activity is going to increase terribly and the United States is going to start suffering some great seismic problems (Ring).

## VOLCANOES

Among the many volcanic eruptions that are going to occur, I saw the one that has just occurred in Hawaii. As I saw the pictures on the television it was really quite uncanny, as I had already seen it taking place during the visions I had seen at the time of my near-death experience.

I was shown many volcanoes erupting around the world. I was told that these activities were due to shifts in the world's axis and would precede many world-shattering events.

I was shown Mt St Helen's eruption. . . . I was also shown other volcanoes. . . . I was shown Mt St Helen's . . . and on May 18, Mt St Helen's really erupted its heaviest. I turned to my husband and said, 'Mt St Helen's just blew its top', and the people there just laughed at me. Later that night we were watching TV and the very scenes that I had seen in my mind were shown on the TV and no one continued to laugh at me then (Ring).

## GEOGRAPHICAL CHANGES

The whole surface of the earth will be changed in the 'twinkling of an eye' just as it says in the Bible. Land will rise up from under the sea and water will rush over the large tracts of land now above sea level. Many people will die at this time, but the earth will be cleansed in the process.

The poles are going to shift. I saw the earth stretching and groaning while giving birth to a new consciousness. I saw that every so often in the history of the world this happens and is inevitable in order for the earth to bring forth a new state of evolution.

I saw that the last time the world faced a similar situation was just before the destruction of Atlantis. Then, as now, people were given plenty of warning that they were disregarding natural and spiritual laws and if they continued to carry on as they were going they would eventually have to face the results of their folly, but they chose to disregard the signs. In the end all but a few who had heeded the warnings perished. It will be the same this time.

There may be a pole shift . . . there are going to be polar changes . . . it's not going to kill all the races off, but we're going to have to start again from square one. . . . There's going to be a larger land mass (Ring).

## METEOROLOGICAL CHANGES

I got a very clear mental picture of drought and famine affecting many lands. Africa is likely to be very badly affected. I also saw a similar situation occurring in a number of Eastern Bloc countries.

There are going to be very severe droughts in many countries. Others are going to suffer from freak storms that will cause tidal waves or flooding to happen as a result of unnaturally heavy rainfalls. . . . All in all, the weather is going to be very unpredictable from now on, in fact these disturbances in the weather patterns have already started.

Oh, my God, that's going to be terrible. The weather is going to go crazy. We're just as likely to have snow in the middle of the summer nowadays as one hundred degree weather. . . . I see droughts in other countries (Ring).

## FOOD SHORTAGES

Because of the violent rape of the earth, acid rain and the general pollution of land and sea, there will be terrible food shortages. All this was caused by man's greed to acquire ever more material wealth at the expense of the quality of life for mankind in general. I saw this selfish attitude, where everyone is only out for themselves and does not care what happens to others, ultimately bringing about the destruction of many people, including the ones whose behaviour had brought this to pass.

There are going to be serious food shortages around the world due to droughts in many places. This will push the price of food up so that many people will have to start going without things that they have always taken for granted.

We'll start getting more droughts, which will bring about shortages in crops and the shortage in crops will cause food prices to rise, which will cause a strain on the economic situation, which is already going downhill. Also at the same time . . . because of the shortage of food and the failing economy, I see a strengthening of arms which causes tension. . . . These kinds of hostilities and [increasing] inflation start more hostilities (Ring).

## ECONOMIC BREAKDOWN

The world economic situation is very unstable. It has now become so complicated that any unexpected event that happens to one country can cause a crisis to develop that affects all countries. I see the cost of production making goods prohibitive and increasing scarcities . . . inflation and increasing unemployment will lead to social unrest and violence that amounts to anarchy.

There will be an illusion of improvement in the general prosperity of the country due to a reshuffling of money and resources. But, I had a feeling that by the end of 1984 another crisis will develop that will have serious repercussions.

## SOCIAL UNREST

I saw a grey miasma spread all over the earth and when I looked I realised it was the vibration of fear that was causing it. Here and there I saw pockets of light coming from enlightened souls who were trying to penetrate the gloom. I saw that this fear was causing the violence and social unrest, also the escalation of the arms race, and that it would only get worse until people learn to overcome fear with love and goodwill toward all men.

I saw riots and men turned against one another in hatred . . . people were afraid to go out.

The problems of social disorder, drugs and violence are going to increase. Unbridled materialism has led to such a state of spiritual impoverishment that people, in seeking a diversion from this feeling of emptiness, are going to be increasingly led to search for kicks in the form of sex, gambling, drink, drugs and violence, leading to ultimate destruction.

## DISEASE

I think that from now on we are likely to hear of many more

strange diseases like AIDS suddenly developing, which doctors don't understand and are unable to cure.

My understanding of the so-called incurable diseases is that they are mostly due to lack of purification within the system and are a reflection in people of the prevailing world conditions. Until the world itself is purified, these conditions are likely to continue to manifest. People seeking a cure need first to be cleansed and purified in mind and body; the healing of the whole organism will then automatically follow.

I got a strong impression that the drug problem is going to get totally out of control.

People talk about the population explosion and the shortage of food as being a threat to life, but I saw a scene in which far more people were destroyed from the effects of drug addiction. This menace threatens to destroy not only the body, as in war and famine, but destroys the soul as well.

To end these various facets of interview material I am including a summary statement from a correspondent of Kenneth Ring's who sent the following account in response to a questionnaire:

The vision of the future I received during my near-death experience was one of tremendous upheaval in the world as a result of our general ignorance of the 'true' reality. I was informed that mankind was breaking the laws of the universe and as a result of this would suffer. This suffering was not due to the vengeance of an indignant God, but rather like the pain one might suffer as a result of arrogantly defying the law of gravity. It was to be an inevitable educational cleansing of the earth, that would creep upon its inhabitants, who would try to hide blindly in the institutions of law, science and religion. Mankind, I was told, was being consumed by the cancers of arrogance, materialism, racism, chauvinism and separatist thinking. I saw sense turning to nonsense, and calamity, in the end, turning to providence. At the end of this general period of transition, mankind was to be 'born anew', with a new sense of his place in the universe. The birth process, however, as in all the kingdoms, was exquisitely painful. Mankind would emerge humbled yet educated, peaceful, and, at last, unified.

It will have become evident by now that all the events intuitively felt and foreseen are interrelated; that the forces impelling both people and nature to such destructive ends are interdependent. One would naturally expect that the geophysical disasters envisaged would bring about the meteorological disruptions that are also seen to occur. This would obviously cause world food shortages which in turn would bring about disruption in the economic systems of the countries affected. All of this would inflame the already growing social unrest, leading to anarchy and economic collapse. In this unbalanced emotional climate it is easy to see how political leaders could be panicked into making the sort of disastrous mistakes that could ultimately lead to a nuclear war.

## NUCLEAR WAR

The messages that have been received by near-death survivors with regard to this possibility are generally felt to be that war is not inevitable, but that there is a very strong likelihood that one might occur towards the end of the 1980s. The other possibility is that a nuclear accident could happen, or that germ warfare will become much more of a threat.

I think towards the end of this decade there is a very grave danger that we will become involved in a Third World War. I would say 1988 is the most likely year for it all to happen.

I feel there is going to be some pact between Russia and a number of Moslem countries which will cause Russia to become involved in a situation affecting them. This will create great tension in the Middle East and, unless the hostilities can be averted, will probably spark off a Third World War.

As time does not exist in the dimension where it is possible for this information to be given and received, it's very difficult to be accurate on this point. But the impression I gained was that the most dangerous time was going to be around 1988.

I think the most likely year for the events I can see arising to take place will be in 1988.

I have a growing conviction that the end of the world is going to come with a whisper and not with a bang. I feel petrified that nobody is protesting about germ warfare as I feel this is how we will go. It won't affect animals. A few people, the innocents [primitive people], will survive in isolated pockets in the Amazon jungles or other places where civilisation has passed by.

It was indicated to me that a nuclear holocaust is now inevitable, as we have transgressed so many of God's laws that it is now impossible for us to avoid the consequences of our actions . . . it will result from the chain of events that we have set in motion.

Well, it'll start in the Middle East . . . and it will be the end. It'll be the Third War (Ring).

It is to be 1988 or was to be. That [would] be the year everything would be wiped away, if we didn't change (Ring).

What I saw was warfare underground tests. And I saw a lot of shake-ups. Seismic activity kicked off by cheaty tests that nobody is admitting. And fallout. . . . The word 'nuclear skirmishes' if one can conceive of such a thing. . . . I saw the aftermath. I saw the explosion places. I saw a chunk of New York City was gone (Ring).

## HOLOCAUST

As well as those who feel that the world is threatened by nuclear disaster, there are those who sense that the holocaust is more likely to be brought about by the forces of nature as a result of the total disregard of the universal laws governing the cosmos and the state of degradation that mankind has fallen into. What follows are some comments from those who feel that humanity is now in imminent peril of experiencing the effects of this folly.

Unless we drastically change the way we are going, I foresee a time of great trial and tribulation ahead. I think we have already unleashed the four horsemen of the Apocalypse.

I was told the earth belongs to God and that no man has a spiritual right to claim bits of it and fight others, either to keep off their bit or try to grab more for themselves. . . . That by doing this we would bring death and destruction to ourselves followed by disease and famine.

I've been told we'll see signs of its approach. . . . There will be great natural catastrophes, an assassination attempt on the Pope, an intensification of the drug problem. Abortion will be legalised. Mercy killings will come to be accepted, both for the senile and for deformed children. Since we've already had most of those signs, I believe the three days of darkness [this respondent's term for the holocaust] will come soon (Ring).

It is generally agreed by almost all the near-death survivors whose experience involved a PV and who subsequently received information pertaining to knowledge gained at the time, that the changes envisaged have probably already begun and are due to reach a climax most commonly thought to occur around 1988 unless some radical change occurs. Those who felt that the events foreseen are now inevitable, nevertheless stressed that, rightly understood, the outcome is both necessary and desirable. Most of the individuals, however, felt that nothing was irrevocable, either with regard to events or timing; and while most agree on the general direction of these events, none of them felt that the unfolding scenario was unalterably fixed. In fact many NDErs stress that events can always be affected by right human action and prayers to God for His intervention. What seems certain is that we appear to be approaching the end of *a* world, but that will not be the end of *the* world. The trials that we are living through are seen by many to be a necessary cleansing from which a new era of peace and universal brotherhood will emerge. Moreover, when this New Age does appear it will then be understood that the devastating changes that preceded it were in fact part of the purgations that were necessary to bring about the transformation of humanity into a new state of being. The quotations included here give an idea of this intention:

The catastrophes will cause tremendous upheavals . . . these have been brought about by a universal decline in ideals and morals. . . . But in the end I see a new world arising from the ashes of the old, in which the Christ consciousness will at last be made manifest and all mankind will dwell together in peace.

I was told that the reason religion was suppressed in Russia is because orthodox religion was felt to do more harm than good. The true spiritual renaissance will come through scientific investigation into ESP and psychic phenomena. Then there will be a religious revival and Russia will lead the world out of the current tensions and crisis.

I saw the world dying, asphyxiated by materialistic greed. As life became more meaningless, I saw crime and mental disease increasing. But after the darkest hour had passed away, during which time all the former things of this world had disintegrated and decayed, I saw a new consciousness emerging and mankind evolving in a new form. Thereafter I beheld a Golden Age in which people would live in love and harmony with each other and all of nature.

These quotations conclude the major elements that comprise the PV scenario. While the messages revealed here will certainly not be acceptable to many people, it must be borne in mind that while the content of these revelations may at first appear alarming, the purpose of their message is not to induce morbid speculation about endless catastrophes, but rather to emphasise that we must all strive towards minimising this aspect in order that the final positive outcome can be brought to fruition. This is the message of hope that these visions contain.

# CHAPTER 9
## *Healing Manifestations*

Verily, verily, I say unto you, he that believeth in me,
the works that I do shall he do also; and greater works
than these shall he do; because I go to the Father.
*The Gospel according to St John*

In addition to the paranormal developments just reviewed, there
is another spectacular manifestation that appears to be spontaneously triggered by the near-death experience, which is the gift
of healing. Like the faculty of clairvoyance, this ability also seems
to be bestowed upon the individuals (in many instances) as a
direct result of their having had a near-death encounter.

It has already been noted in the chapter on after-effects that one
of the changes which often occurs after an NDE relates to a very
powerful motivation to be of service to others. It seems that this
aspiration or prayer is granted in accordance with the latent
potential capabilities of each individual: while some people may
be directed to serve the community by developing their ability to
tune into consciousness in order to be able to advance certain
specific diagnostic talents and so advise on matters of health,
others will be enabled to work for the benefit of mankind in a
different way by using their newly acquired healing abilities in a
more direct manner.

Just as each epoch brings about its own conditions and
attendant problems, so it also always provides individuals who,
by applying new perspectives to the prevailing circumstances, are
able to meet the challenge of their age. These individuals find
systems for understanding and explaining the emerging concepts
of reality by having the courage to rise above the accepted
standards of the day, thereby often drawing upon themselves the
ridicule and scorn of their contemporaries, which only their faith
in God and their unconditional love for humanity enables them to
endure.

Today, when both physical and psychological disorders are

134

increasing at an alarming rate, people are seeking for alternative approaches to health in ever-increasing numbers. Disillusioned by the old methods of treating symptoms (which usually has the effect of masking or suppressing the problem so that it often appears again later in a more virulent form), they are turning to people who see the body as part of a total organism which acts as a unified whole and who by seeking to remove the cause of the 'dis-ease' are able to restore the organism to harmonious function again.

It is well known among the practitioners of what have come to be known as New Age paradigms of health, that well-being comes from a body-mind matrix and cannot be applied merely through the agency of injections or prescriptions. Those working in the field of holistic health know that until psychological and somatic unison is achieved the problem is unlikely to be resolved. What is more, until the spiritual dimension is also recognised and taken into consideration, a really big breakthrough in the treatment of many diverse disorders will never be fully accomplished. But great strides are being made and what now seems certain is that, largely due to the pioneering efforts of these enlightened individuals, the former preoccupation with disease is now giving way to an understanding of the dynamics of health. In *The Aquarian Conspiracy* Marilyn Ferguson quotes an anatomist as saying, 'The healer inside us is the wisest, most complx, integrated entity in the universe', and she goes on to add that, 'In a sense, we know now, there is always a doctor in the house.'

The physician within usually seems to be more readily accessible to those individuals who have had a 'core experience' during their NDE, and people who report awareness of this phenomenon often observe that it is as if they are able to tune into a state of universal consciousness and power whenever the need to help others arises. As with the other paranormal developments, sometimes the information, which in this case pertains to methods of obtaining cures for certain diseases, is given at the time of the NDE itself, but more often individuals state that they discover they are possessed of this ability some time after recovery from their near-death event.

## PROCEDURE

In order to include this aspect of NDEs I found that it was necessary to conduct a special search for such cases. The result is that the material presented in this chapter is decidedly selective and my procedure for obtaining samples was inclined to be rather haphazard. Also, because the number of cases was very small, it was not possible for me to undertake any statistical analysis at the time. But, as was the case with the instances of precognitive and prophetic visions, I feel (in agreement with Kenneth Ring) that in view of the essentially significant nature of the material it justifies my including it as it stands. All things considered though, it is necessary to bear in mind that the information presented here has been specially sought out and that this fact, taken together with the very limited size of my sample, means the material would need to be further validated before any conclusions could rightly be justified. These cases dealing with spiritual and psychic healing, both during and after an NDE and also with the development of subsequent healing abilities, have not been described elsewhere in similar studies, nor has information about it been published before as far as I am aware.

## CASE HISTORY MATERIAL

### Spiritual Healing

In cases where healing of the illness that brought about the NDE takes place, these instances always occur within the context of the NDE (i.e. during the encounter with the individual's guide or the being of light who is often taken to be Jesus), and respondents usually assert that it was their guides or the being of light who healed them at that time. Occasionally, though, healing of the illness will take place subsequent to recovery from the near-death crisis.

A case that serves to illustrate several of these features was provided by an American respondent. His near-death crisis resulted from cancer. During his NDE he was met by a being who healed him of his disease. In particular he remembered:

Suddenly I seemed to be right in front of the being standing there. He was standing with the light behind him and I had the dark behind me, so I was actually facing the light. I came up to within what seemed like about a foot away from his face. . . . I looked at this being and there was just enough light on his face for me to tell that it was what I took to be an elder person. I could see the wrinkles around his eyes, he had a long, straight face, no beard, but piercing eyes and white hair. I was not aware if he had a robe on or what he was wearing, only that he was looking right through me. He – I was trying to make up my mind who he was; I know it was Christ, but I had always been led to believe that Christ was a young man with a beard etc., so I was debating with myself. I was sure it was Him yet he did not look like I thought he should look. As he stood looking at me his eyes seemed to be shooting fire right through me. He was not smiling, but as he looked at me he said the following: 'That's enough, it's dead, it's gone.' His words were ringing in my ears. At that I started to move back again the way I had come, in the opposite direction, going towards the hospital. . . . I don't remember how I got back to the hospital room or into my body. I only remember going through the dark. I mulled over what had happened. In my own mind, I don't know what he meant by 'That's enough'; to this day I don't know what he meant. People have suggested I had suffered enough, but I felt that I had suffered hardly at all by comparison with someone who has been badly burnt or smashed up in an automobile accident. But I do know what he meant when he said, 'It's dead.' To me it meant that the germ was dead. It's gone, I no longer have leukaemia.

He further added this gratifying follow-up comment:

At any rate I had been given a maximum of two years to live by the doctors. . . . It's now six years since I had the experience and there has been no recurrence of the cancer, so it looks as if it's cleared.

The next case concerns an Englishman whose account also exemplifies many of the characteristic features which are encountered during a spiritual healing. His NDE occurred five days after a very severe abdominal operation. While he was still unconscious, complications set in and his wife was notified that he was dying. During this time he had the following experience:

> My next feeling was of lying on the bed, physically my first feeling since collapsing, and an entity clothed in a coloured cloak, [of] indescribably beautiful colours, and a brightness most intense. This something stood at the right-hand side of my head, two hands were lightly placed on my body, slowly moved down to my feet, and up the left side, pausing at my head, then was gone. I have no recollection of anything until next day. From then I made a very rapid recovery and was soon back with my family.

Another aspect that can occur during this phase of the NDE concerns information pertaining to the illness itself, which is sometimes given to the individual at the same time as the healing takes place in order that the knowledge can be disseminated for the benefit of others who are suffering from the same type of illness. Referring to this aspect the respondent who was cured of leukaemia said:

> As I was leaving him [the being thought to be Christ] I had the impression that he was trying to impress on me by mental telepathy, or whatever you want to call it, that the way to cure cancer was to heat the body up to kill the germ, then cool the body off to get rid of it and that I was to tell a specific doctor and a nurse, that this was the way to cure leukaemia. This was the only thing he communicated to me. . . . For a long time I couldn't bring myself to talk about it, but weeks or maybe months later, I got the doctor in the room and said, 'I know how to cure leukaemia', and told him what I had been told to tell. My wife and kids who were in the room at the time, along with the doctor, thought I was going out of my mind or something at this point, so I don't know if anything was ever done.

### Psychic Healing

The second feature referred to concerns healing that will sometimes take place subsequent to recovery from a near-death crisis. This was the case with an English woman whose NDE resulted from the very prolonged birth of her daughter. She recounted this incident:

> I was in bed feeling drowsy when suddenly I found myself floating above my bed. I was in a horizontal position about two feet above my bed. I don't remember seeing my body in bed or being aware that I was out of my body. I seemed to be lying on some sort of operating table or doctors' examination table. There were about four or five men in white coats standing round me who appeared to be working on me, they seemed to be performing some kind of psychic surgery. I asked them what they were doing and they said, 'We have come to adjust something.' I don't know what it was. They also said, 'Something needed to be reactivated.' they carried on for what seemed like about ten or fifteen minutes; it's very hard to tell as the whole episode had a timeless feel to it. When they were finished, I slowly drifted back down on to my bed again and they slowly faded from sight. They left one of the white-coated men behind who stood behind my head with his hands on my head. I got the impression he was giving me some sort of healing. I felt warm and drowsy and had an incredible sense of well-being. I don't remember any more as at this point I drifted off into a very deep and peaceful sleep. A few days later I noticed I had developed a slight discharge and as I could not imagine what was causing it I went to see my doctor. After examining me he said there was nothing wrong, but for some reason the glands had become ACTIVATED and that they would settle down again in time. He said it was lucky for me it had happened spontaneously like this, as I had been having problems due to my glands not functioning properly. He said he could not understand how it had happened, but added that these things did sometimes occur and that there was no way to account for it.

The three cases presented here give us a fascinating glimpse of a phenomenon that has so far not been explored, providing us with tentative information concerning what I have chosen to term spiritual and psychic healing respectively in order to distinguish them from one another. Clearly, this aspect is one that is deserving of further investigation and if more research was undertaken could well yield information that would give us additional insights into our understanding of NDEs in general.

## Healing abilities

The next category of healing manifestations I want to examine is the ability to heal others through the agency of prayer and the 'laying on of hands'. The man who returned from death to find himself in the mortuary has ample opportunity to serve humanity through his work in the Church Army. Since his NDE he has dedicated himself to this evangelistic mission with a 'new urgency, a new authority'. What follows are a number of quotes relating to his ability to heal:

> Alfred was dying, so I was told when I visited him in hospital, but after prayer and the laying on of hands in the name of the Lord he made a complete recovery and is still alive many years later.

> Stanley was bedfast and he and his wife thought he was dying, but following a laying on of hands he was up and about the house within hours.

> Delia was in a coma when I visited her in hospital. The ward sister had little hope for her and her family were worried to distraction about her. I prayed over and laid hands upon her unconscious body. Next day she was conscious, alert and on the way to recovery, and, in fact, she became fitter than she had been for years.

He also refers to another aspect of his gift which allows him to recognise that 'death, unlike disease, is not necessarily contrary to God's will for us'. And he further adds, 'He has made us finite. Though my earthly body is precious to God, it is His will that one day I shall discard it.' This conviction has given him the ability to recognise that there is a right time to go, as well as realising that many of us go before our intended time due to negative conditions that come about as a result of our breaking the laws governing life. Below, he recalls two cases where he was able to help someone, whose time had evidently come, to let go and pass peacefully over:

> Amy [was] a lovely gentle old lady whose body was wracked
> with an advanced gas gangrene condition. She was in
> constant pain and many would have died long before she
> did, but as the doctor told her family, she had a strong and
> vigorous heart and there seemed no prospect other than that
> of weeks of continuing agony ahead of her. Her family
> called me in. They told me that neither she, nor they, were
> afraid of death. 'If only she could pass away quickly and
> quietly. . . .', they said. I laid on hands in the Lord's name
> and prayed for his healing intervention. Amy was dead
> within hours.

> Or there was Judith who had a brain tumour. The doctor
> said she would live for about a fortnight of agony. I laid on
> hands and prayed and again she was dead in hours.

Finally, he reported an incident which has a correlation with the
case of spiritual healing which has been quoted. It concerns a
woman who was dying of cancer. I have not been able to ascertain
whether the woman had an NDE at the time of her experience, but
it seems quite probable. The account is as follows:

> Emma was supposed to have terminal cancer, but she told
> me that the Lord had appeared to her in a dream and told her
> she would not die. He gave her a simple action to perform –
> rather like Naaman washing in the River Jordan [2 Kings
> 5:10] – and she did it obediently and trustingly. To the
> astonishment of her consultant the cancer vanished without
> trace. She is still alive many years later.

In the case of the man who was healed by the entity robed in a
brilliant cloak of rainbow hues, we have another instance which
demonstrates this ability, and at the same time shows the growing
realisation of evidence of this gift. Following recovery from his
near-death crisis he became aware that certain exceptional events
were taking place:

> Then many unusual incidents occurred. The first that I recall
> was: I came home from one of my business trips to find our
> pet [cat] was in a terrible condition, foaming at the mouth,

shaking all over, could not stand, lifeless. I nursed her for the evening, made up the fire for the night, and left her on an old piece of blanket in front of the fire, expecting that she would die during the night. To my surprise, I found her next morning bright and cheerful as if nothing had ever been wrong.

Another time I had reason to run out into the garden and a twig of a tree stuck in my eye. Without thought I pulled the end of the twig from my eye and clasped my face. Taking my hands away, to my astonishment, no blood or pain, and looking into a mirror, no sign of any injury.

Another time I was making some home-made wine, and was pouring three gallons of boiling water on to the mush, when a couple of friends called. Whilst talking and carrying on with the job, I put my hands and arms into the water and began stirring. One of my friends shouted at me, and I, suddenly aware of what I had done, pulled my hands out of the water, and was amazed to find that there was no pain, scalding or blisters.

He went on to recall: 'Several such incidents happened, but I still didn't register that something was happening; I still didn't accept these many incidents; I was vague about them.' Then one day an incident occurred that finally made him realise that something very unusual had taken place in him since his NDE. He explained it in this way:

One evening I was talking to a friend and his wife who had been deaf in one ear since childhood, when he suddenly asked me to put my hands on his wife's faulty ear. In a minute or two, taking my hands away, she said, 'I can hear!'

The result of this spectacular incident was that for the first time he began to give thought to and recognised that he had been given the gift of healing. He then went on to relate that he has since that time become a 'practising healer' and has for the past twenty-eight years devoted his life to this end, in the certain knowledge that he has been given this ability to serve others, 'with the wonderful inner joy of having helped thousands'.

The last case from my British sample to be presented in which this healing ability is demonstrated relates to a woman who developed manifestations of both clairvoyant and healing gifts. Her NDE occurred during an operation for the removal of her womb, and she has already been quoted before in the course of this work. In her case the person requiring healing does not have to be in her presence for a healing to occur, as there is no laying on of hands. Rather, she has the gift of being able to 'see' clairvoyantly, not only the disease itself, but also the cause of the problem. She is further able to send her healing powers by 'remote control', distance seeming to be no barrier to her ability to cast out unwanted manifestations. She does not go into a trance on these occasions, nor does she need to put herself into a state of self-induced hypnotic slumber. She is fully conscious while working and only requires that an atmosphere of peace and tranquillity prevail to allow her to be able to concentrate or meditate on the problem with the utmost intensity. The two examples given below serve to illustrate the extraordinary powers that have developed in this woman since she underwent her NDE.

In the first instance a woman of middle age was sent by her doctor to have a check-up as she had not had one for many years. During the examination it was discovered that she had a lump in one of her breasts. She was told that she would have to go into hospital as soon as possible to have it attended to, so an appointment was made for her to have this done within six weeks from the time of the diagnosis. She rang the healer (whom we will call Irene) in an absolute panic. Irene was very reassuring and told her not to worry as all would be well. All she asked was that the woman seeking help should link with her in thought four times a day for half an hour, at eight o'clock in the morning, at noon, at six o'clock in the evening, and again at about ten o'clock at night, just before she went to bed. The very day that she started to receive healing treatment this woman told me that she was sitting quietly at home when something very unusual happened. It was shortly after ten in the evening and she was meditating, linking in thought with Irene, when suddenly she was 'aware of a light in the corner of the room which grew brighter and brighter, and when it hit me I was sent sprawling across the sofa on which I was sitting'. She said that during the next few days she was aware of changes taking place in her body. The following morning she telephoned Irene and told her what had happened. Irene replied, 'that was just the first impact, it will not hit you so hard in future, but we will continue sending the healing four times a day.' A few weeks later she went to the hospital, as arranged to have a further examination. When the doctor could find no evidence of a lump, he turned to his patient and said 'What do you think has happened?' She replied, 'I knew you were going to ask me that, because I knew it had dispersed as a result of the spiritual healing I have been receiving.' He was evidently rather scornful of this remark and said, 'If you like to believe in things like that it's up to you, but these things can disappear of their own accord.'

The second example concerns a young girl who had suffered a breakdown and was in a psychiatric hospital following a psychotic episode in which she had become completely deranged. Again Irene was consulted, this time by the distracted mother who was at her wit's end. She was also reassured and told not to worry as everything would be all right. About ten days after the treatment commenced, the mother was paying one of her frequent visits to her daughter, when she noticed to her joy that a singular change had occurred and that the girl seemed to be her old happy self again, running to greet her mother with affection. Upon inquiring what had brought about this change, the girl said,

> Well it's funny really, because I suddenly felt a very strong urge to go and sit quietly by myself in the sun-room, when all of a sudden I felt as if someone had hit me hard in the back. In fact it almost knocked me off my chair. After that I started to feel much better.

The girl made a rapid recovery and was allowed home shortly afterwards.

When I inquired of Irene what had transpired during the course of healing, she said that in both cases she had some difficulty in 'getting through', as something in both of them was rather resistant to the changes that needed to take place before healing could be accomplished. She said that in these cases she 'literally had to throw the power at them in order to ensure that it hit the spot!' In the first case the impact was felt in the chest and in the second in the back, which in this case was the site of the problem, as the imbalance was due to a malfunction located in the central nervous system in the spinal column.

The ability to perform healing miracles through the agency of spiritual or psychic intervention is, of course, not new. The Bible gives us many examples of such occurrences in the Old and New Testaments, and accounts of the supernatural powers of both Christian Saints and Eastern mystics attest to healing abilities involving paranormal means. But why should people who have had an NDE be among the likely candidates for inclusion in this select brotherhood? What is the common denominator that links this remarkable ability (which has long been the province of certain outstanding men and women down the ages) with the NDEr of today? It seems to me that these abilities are a natural by-product of a heightened state of spiritual awareness which is usually accompanied by moral elevation and a selfless desire to use their newly acquired powers for the benefit of others.

The fact that many of those who devote their lives to this cause find their own health improving and their vitality increased is not surprising when one considers that they are themselves recharged by the power that flows through them. But there is also another aspect that has a bearing on this phenomenon, which relates to a cosmic law whereby we are in reality all part of one another, and that what you wish for another you will yourself receive. It seems from the records of those who have been healed that people who pray for others to be helped, rather than asking for themselves, are invariably more likely to receive healing than those who pray for themselves alone.

There has long been a tradition among occultists that misuse of these powers for selfish reasons motivated by greed or a desire for personal gain (e.g. money or fame) is attended by severe penalties, not the least of which being that these abilities are no longer effective. This has led certain people in the past to resort to fraud in order to keep up appearances, thus giving those organisations with whom these people have been associated an undeservedly bad name, as a lot of valuable work is done by many self-effacing people of goodwill who quietly work behind the scenes and seek no personal reward, other than the joy that comes from helping others.

When the channel to cosmic knowledge is free from self-aggrandisement, which has the effect of blocking the flow, many miracles are possible that are able to cure both bodily ills and problematical material conditions. For nowhere are we told that impoverishment of any sort is the will of the Father, and we only have to look around us at Mother Nature to see the evident manifestations of abundance. Rather we are told not to put the gods of money, fame and power above Him, but that we should first 'Seek the Kingdom of Heaven' and that all these things will then be added unto us.

# CHAPTER 10
# *Evolutionary aspects of near-death experiences*

> So shalt thou feed on Death, that feeds on men:
> and Death once dead, there's no more dying then.
> *Shakespeare*

I have now come to the final feature that is sometimes noted as an after-effect of the NDE. It has been observed to occur more frequently in those individuals whose experience has alerted them to the inherent possibilities of actively attempting to achieve union with their divine nature and who therefore strive to further their spiritual development to this end, than in cases where no further progress is consciously undertaken. The result of this effort is that a psycho-physiological transformation is often induced which, when allowed to progress to completion, leads to a spiritual and psychic rebirth.

There are a number of different methods whereby this is possible and which in recent years have become the focus of much interest in the West, although various systems for attaining this legendary state have been described for thousands of years in the ancient Vedas and other mystical works of the East. In the case of people who have had an NDE, though, the process seems to be more instinctive and can even be unconsciously undertaken. They do not usually seek external direction, as they are more likely than others to be instructed by their inner guides, who lead them slowly, surely and safely along the path towards enlightenment.

For the rest, the methods of attempting to achieve this elevated state vary according to the technique chosen, which is usually the preferred method of the master or guru whose teaching the individual decides to follow. One such practice is known as Kundalini Yoga, which involves the attempt to activate the latent force that is known to reside at the base of the spine, and the

philosophy attending it is one in which the human body is seen as
a reflection of the whole cosmos with the spinal column as the
Axis Mundi. Kundalini is always pictured as a serpent lying coiled
in sleep at the base of this column and is identified with the life
force or sexual energy, the two being merely seen as different
aspects of the same power. The aim of arousing this dormant
power is to cause it to ascend this column, passing through a
number of centres (known as chakras), before reaching the brain
where it is united with superconscious forces.

One of the reasons that this process was so little understood or
accepted in the West until recently, despite the fact that it has been
referred to in Christian mystical texts as well as Eastern treatises
since earliest times, was largely because the methods employed by
various esoteric sects that engaged in the practice were always
closely guarded by initiates. These initiates realised the inherent
dangers in a technique that, if practised by individuals who were
not spiritually and psychologically prepared, could do more harm
than good. Even so, the symptoms were (and still are) often
mistaken for insanity, largely because the experience is not
properly understood in the light of its outcome.

Probably the best documented case of kundalini phenomena to
be studied this century is that of Gopi Krishna. When we consider
what he has to say about the effects of the experience it is easy to
see the correlation between the events that occur during an NDE
and those brought about by the practice of this system of
meditation. One can also readily understand why a person, once
having undergone such an experience, would willingly subject
himself to an activity that would enable him to repeat this
transforming event. Referring to the nature of his mystical
experience in his book *Higher Consciousness*, Gopi Krishna
states:

> In the majority of cases the experience lasts for only a brief
> duration. In may occur gradually as the result of Yoga or
> other spiritual practices or it may come spontaneously to
> one entirely unprepared for it. In either case the impact is
> stunning, and the ecstatic feels himself torn from his
> moorings and face to face with an experience totally foreign
> to him. It may sometimes take a visionary aspect, involving
> the form of a Divine Being in glory, or in a Divine order of

things. Or one may find oneself transported to other spheres and other-worldly realms.

In the genuine experience the characteristic symptoms are: (1) sensation of light, which can be both internal and external. The subject feels as if a wondrous effulgence has illuminated his interior and maybe even the objects in the outside world. The sensation is at times so realistic as to give the impression of an inner and outer conflagration; (2) an overwhelming sense of wonder and awe; (3) unshakable conviction about the reality of the experience; (4) a sense of infinitude and unbounded knowledge; (5) certainty of immortality; (6) intellectual illumination; (7) a vivid feeling of encounter with an inexpressible, all-knowing Intelligence of an omniscient Divine Being; (8) a flood of pure emotion, an overwhelming feeling of devotion, reverence, submission, love and adoration, cascading tears, or hair standing on end.

Whether the experience is of a visionary type or unattended by visions and appearances, the most amazing feature lies in the alteration experienced in one's own personality and channels of observation. The observer finds himself transformed. He is no longer the puny, fear-ridden individual, unsure about the nature of his being and destiny. He either realises himself as a widely stretched, floating mass of consciousness, released from the bondage of flesh, or he finds himself face to face with a celestial being, resplendent and sublime. Or he may see himself surrounded by a superearthly scene of unequalled beauty and grandeur. In almost every case the vision is unlike anything experienced on earth in the ordinary course of life. This feature is so striking that it sharply divides mystical experience from anything seen in dreams or witnessed under drugs.

As the foregoing passage could quite easily be taken for a description of a 'core experience' it will be interesting to note whether other similarities exist in a comparison of the two sets of circumstances that lead up to this event.

It has already been noted that in the near-death event the 'core experience' usually takes place at that moment when there is a temporary cessation of heartbeat and respiratory activity. In cases of induced mystical experience this phenomenon can also be observed to occur and indeed is considered by some teachers to be a necessary prerequisite for arresting the metabolic process in order to bring about the desired experience. Referring to this ability, Paramhansa Yogananda has observed that it is considered expedient for the yogi to learn to 'release the life force from his heart' in order to bring it under control, but he adds that when the life force is withdrawn from the body it 'appears "dead" or motionless and rigid'. He points out that the yogi is fully aware of his bodily condition of 'suspended animation', but reveals that as he progresses to higher states he is able to commune with God without bodily fixation in his 'ordinary waking consciousness, even in the midst of exacting wordly duties'. He further quotes his own guru, Sri Yukteswar, as saying:

> The ancient yogis discovered that the secret of cosmic consciousness is intimately linked with breath mastery. . . . The life force, which is ordinarily absorbed in maintaining the heart pump, must be freed for higher activities by a method of stilling the ceaseless demands of the breath.

By now it must be starting to become evident to the reader that there is a definite connection between the biological process that attends death and the one that is necessary to reach higher states of consciousness. In both cases this state is attained by the withdrawal of the life force away from bodily sensation. Where this process is deliberately induced it is achieved by a method of centring inwardly the life currents away from the sensory world; in this way the adept is able to simulate a death-like state that enables him to experience union with the Christ Consciousness.

It would seem reasonable to expect that such a fantastic event, involving as it does both bodily trauma and a radical trans-formation in consciousness, would bring about great evolu-tionary changes in mind and body. This does indeed seem to be the case, for apart from the after-effects in personality and the value changes that have already been discussed, it has been noted that in many cases a number of very unusual physiological changes also seem to occur following the experience. It is, moreover, evident that the NDE does not simply remain an isolated incident in the life of the experiencer, spectacular though this experience may have been, but rather it activates a process that often lasts many years, during which time symptom patterns and bodily sensations are revealed that have also been noted in similar accounts recorded by Christian mystics and yoga adepts alike.

These symptoms are many and varied, but underlying them all is a movement towards the purification and transformation of the entire organism which is set in motion by this 'divine energy'. For, in its rise towards the crown centre, this life force must pass through various centres, which are thought to be associated with all the important organs of the body, in order to enable them to be 'opened' or vivified. Whenever this energy meets resistance (which occurs when a centre is 'blocked'), the central nervous system appears to become involved in an attempt to throw off this stress. In its upward path this force, when prevented from flowing freely, evidently begins to act of its own volition, engaging in a process of slowly spreading throughout the entire psycho-physiological system while modifying the biological structure of the vital body current.

The kind of manifestations that are most generally associated with this process, and which are likely to be encountered when this energy is obstructed, include: abnormal breathing patterns and muscular spasms or involuntary body movements, which can be readily verified; sensations described as headaches and backaches, itching, tingling or vibrating; fluctuations in body temperature and feelings of bodily expansion and contraction. Others include unusual mental processes which can cause a sense of detachment and disassociation, with apparent distortion of the cognitive processes and sometimes extremes of emotional feeling such as ecstasy, bliss, peace, love and joy, occasionally also intense fear, anxiety, depression, hatred and confusion. Generally this intensity of feeling is more likely to be experienced in the early stages of the process. Later, when the obstructions to progress have been worked through, contentment and a sense of cosmic harmony are more likely to predominate.

I know of no study that has been undertaken in this country that has investigated these symptoms in the light of possible kundalini manifestations, or which has sought to distinguish these symptoms from those of pathology. It seems that many people undergoing what is in reality an exceptionally creative process (but which can be very difficult to live through), turn to professional people for help only to be classified as psychotic and given drugs to suppress the symptoms. This makes matters worse as it further blocks the process, which in turn increases the severity of the symptoms.

As with all the other categories that are examined in the second part of this book, which did not form part of my original thesis investigation, I have not undertaken any systematic research and my observations have mostly been made in the course of my practice. The result is that I am obliged of necessity to offer my material in the form of case history studies, which is actually my preferred method of presentation.

Shortly after completing the first draft of this book I was presented with a copy of *Heading Towards Omega*, a new book by Kenneth Ring, subtitled *In Search of the Meaning of the Near-Death Experience*. In it he reports on his research into the biological basis of NDEs. His findings are almost identical to my own and support those put forward in a very interesting small book entitled *Kundalini – Psychosis or Transcendence?*, which was written a few years ago by Lee Sannella, an American psychiatrist who examined the effects of kundalini manifestations on people who had taken up meditation. The observations in both works are very similar to those that I have noted both as a post-NDE effect and also in clients who have been referred to me as supposedly suffering from an apparent psychosis, but who in fact did not conform to the classic symptoms. These people were obviously going through a period of transformation and, apart from often being extremely psychic, almost always had a clear sense of reality regarding their situation and generally had great insight into what was happening to them, unlike the typical psychotic. In referring to these cases, Dr Sannella suggests:

> There are many undergoing this process who at times feel quite insane. When they behave well and keep silent they may avoid being called schizophrenic, or being hospitalised, or sedated. Nevertheless their isolation and sense of separation from others may cause them much suffering.

He further adds: 'Certainly we must no longer subject people, who might be in the midst of a re-birth process, to drugs or shock therapies, approaches which are at opposite poles to creative self-development.

So far, I have tried to describe the overall manifestations that can arise in different men and women when this evolutionary force is activated, whether deliberately or spontaneously (as often seems to be the case in NDEs), in order to show something of the uniformity of signs and symptoms that can indicate its presence. I now propose to examine each of these different characteristics separately and in turn give examples delineating details which show how the effects of this process manifest, so as to deepen the reader's understanding of its objective indications and subjective descriptions. Several of the factors that I will be discussing here refer to qualities that have already been identified by Dr Sannella and constitute part of his study of the kundalini process.

In the summary of signs and symptoms which he discusses in his book, Sannella separated these two factors into four basic categories: (a) motor, (b) sensory, (c) interpretive, and (d) non-physiological. The first he describes as 'Any manifestations which can be independently observed and physically measured'; the second as 'Inner sensations such as lights, sounds and experiences, normally classed as sensations'; the third as 'Mental processes which interpret experience'; and the fourth as 'Phenomena which taken at face value as genuine occurrences, must involve factors for which physiological explanations are not sufficient'. He points out that although this four-fold classsification was made for convenience, in actual fact the symptoms in different categories (i.e. abnormal breathing, bodily sensations, or intense psychic experiences) 'may often be merely different aspects of a single integrated experience', which is also generally true of all NDE phenomena. Another difficulty which he points out, and which I also experienced, is that some manifestations can be encountered in more than one category at the same time. Taking his summary as a model for cross-cultural comparison, I propose to use his analysis of components as a basis for surveying the recurrent features. What now follows are descriptions of these characteristics.

### Abnormal breathing patterns

This is one of the classic ways of inducing mystical states and is widely known in India under the name of pranayama, which means breath control. It is a psycho-physiological method

whereby the blood is decarbonised and recharged with oxygen.
Yogananda says of this practice:

> The atoms of this extra oxygen are converted into life
> currents to rejuvenate the brain and spine centres. By
> stopping the accumulation of venous blood, the yogi is able
> to lessen or prevent the decay of tissues; the advanced yogi
> transmutes his cells into pure energy.

Today, growing awareness of a condition known as the
hyperventilation syndrome has recently attracted the attention of
a number of physicians, notably Peter Nixon, who is the Senior
Consultant Cardiologist at Charing Cross Hospital. The physiological effects of this condition can relate to virtually any organ
or system and its variety of symptoms can range from thyroid,
cardiac, gastro-intestinal, or respiratory, to central nervous
disorders. Aside from some indications that disturbing psychic
ailments can frequently occur, there appears to have been little
systematic research into this aspect which prompted L.C. Lum
(1981), in his informative paper 'Hyperventilation and anxiety
states', to observe that 'medical awareness indeed generally stops
short at the "hysterical fit".' These abnormal breathing patterns
have been observed to mimic spontaneously the classic pranayama exercises: rapid breathing, shallow breathing, deep
breathing or prolonged retention of breath. This spontaneous
occurrence is however, quite normal according to yoga theory
and is likely to happen fairly regularly in the process of kundalini
awakening. There is a warning though, to the effect that
deliberate practice of pranayama in order to accelerate this
process by untutored individuals can be dangerous, as well as being
unnecessary, as this force will arise of itself as part of the natural
process of evolution. The effects are very similar to those of a 'core
experience', and most descriptions emphasise the peace, beauty
and sense of transcendence associated with the experience. A few
brief quotes will illustrate the strength of these feelings:

> All fear and pain were gone. I was calm and everything was
> very bright.

> The effects of hyperventilating can make you feel awful, but
> then suddenly there comes a moment when it is really
> beautiful.

Suddenly all the pain and fear were gone and I felt peaceful and warm.

The room suddenly seemed to be flooded with sunlight and I felt a wonderful glow surrounding me.

It was a beautiful feeling There was this beautiful light and I felt warm and uplifted.

As can be seen, the testimony of hyperventilators does not differ from that of other accounts of NDEs or mystical experience. Furthermore, the effects of this abnormal breathing pattern on the physiological system noted by clinical observation describes in similar terms to those of Yogananda the causative mechanism whereby this condition is brought about. For it 'acts by blowing off excessive quantities of carbon dioxide thus producing respiratory alkalosis', resulting in the low levels of carbon dioxide that have been noted to occur in relation to those circumstances.

### Muscular spasms or involuntary body movements

These can involve cramp-like sensations that are relatively mild or muscular spasms which may be more pronounced, even resembling epilepsy if the nervous system is particularly sensitive, as often happens in the early stages of a physio-kundalini awakening. In this case the manifestations may be accompanied by insensibility or impairment of consciousness, which is commonly attended by peculiar convulsive seizures. It is interesting to note that the well-known American psychic Edgar Cayce suffered from these seizures as a boy, which were diagnosed as epilepsy. He is also reported to have had mystical experiences in which a 'figure in white bright as the Noonday light' appeared to him. This experience seems to have been followed by feelings of disorientation and an inability to concentrate, but righted itself when his renowned gift began to manifest. What seems certain is that these pathological symptoms invariably disappear once a creative outlet directed towards selfless activity is found for the psychic energies generated by this process. The ensuing quotations will serve to show the kind of sensations that are described:

Every now and then my hands seem to start vibrating with energy. They also go all mottled and become quite rigid. The fingers then become slightly curled up like this [she showed me what happens], as if I'm holding an invisible ball.

Sometimes I wake up in the night and I am absolutely rigid. I cannot move. It's quite frightening really, as I am unable to cry out for help, but after a little while it passes and I am back to normal again.

Then I began to get cramps in my feet and legs, which was followed by vibrations. I also noticed the big toenail on my left foot had turned black, which was strange because I didn't remember having banged it or dropped anything on it.

At times I seem to go into a trance-like state and am aware at the same time of waves of energy going through my body which causes jerking and twitching over which I have no control. It only lasts a few minutes and I feel none the worse afterwards. I went to see my doctor, but he was not very sympathetic and I got the impression he regarded me as rather neurotic. He gave me some pills, but they made me feel so dreadful that I stopped taking them. Since then I have developed many psychic abilities and I find I am able to help others. I find now my mediumship has developed I no longer get these attacks.

These symptoms were observed in the well-attested case of St Teresa of Lisieux who, as a young girl, shortly after being admitted to the local convent, was assailed by convulsions which seemed to emanate from some strange force. She also appeared to swoon during which time her body became rigid, but she always maintained that she was fully aware even when apparently in a coma. At the time, she was regularly attended by a capable physician who, although baffled by her condition and unable to alleviate her symptoms, nevertheless confirmed that it could in no way be attributed to 'hysteria'.

## *Headaches or pains in the head*

These are sometimes reported as migraines and seem more likely to affect the left side of the body. The eyes and neck may become involved in the manifestations. These headaches are often of sudden onset and without apparent reason, usually ceasing as abruptly as they began. The cause seems linked to an obstruction in the flow of energy, due to a centre not yet being opened sufficiently, so that a build-up of psychic force causing pressure results. During this process there often seems to be a corresponding condition (i.e. obstruction to progress) which is made manifest in the outer world at the same time, in order that the individual can be given an opportunity of overcoming an interrelated psychological block, thereby fulfilling the old adage 'as without, so within'. For once the situation is accepted, it becomes possible to surrender to 'divine will' and fear in the form of resistance is overcome.

A striking example of this occurred to a woman who suffered from these migraine type headaches during the period following her NDE while she was developing spiritual awareness of her life conditions. She said that while she was going through this process she found herself:

> Totally bereft of everyone and everything that mattered to me. Finally utterly alone (even my beloved little dog, my only companion, was taken from me) and without hope, I faced financial ruin. My greatest need had always been emotional and financial security and my greatest fear up to that time had been of finding myself without these things. For a while all my energy was directed towards trying desperately to hang on to my old structure, as I feared I would be utterly destroyed if I 'let go'. The power of the psychic energy which I directed to my arms for the effort of 'hanging on' resulted in both my shoulders becoming 'frozen', a very painful condition. Finally, one day I realised I could not hang on any longer, so I faced the worst. Mentally I 'saw' myself out on the street with a small suitcase which contained all my wordly goods, having lost my home and all my possessions. I asked myself how I felt and was amazed to find that I felt completely free. I reasoned

that as there was no one in my life I was not responsible for anyone, therefore I could go where I pleased and do as I liked. I also realised that my possessions were in reality possessing me and in fact there is no such thing as material security. I saw too that if I had nothing then I had nothing to lose. Providing I didn't ruin my health with unnecessary worry I was free as a bird to explore the whole world and choose from among the many opportunities that life always offers to those who seek for them. I also saw that living meant moving out into the mainstream of life with its rapids, shallows and obstacles to be circumvented. That by staying in a backwater where there was no movement, the water became stagnant, and stagnant water is unable to support life. So I said out loud to the 'boys upstairs', whoever you are I hope you know what you're doing because I don't have a clue what's going on. But I give in, 'not my will but thine be done'. I surrender to the 'divine will' and accept what is. That night I slept like a baby and within a few days everything changed. The money I needed to save my situation unexpectedly arrived from an unlikely source and was exactly the amount I needed, no more, no less. People started coming into my life and offering all kinds of help, new opportunities started to open up and within a very short while my shoulders returned to normal (without the use of drugs) as the energy that had become frozen there thawed out.

This case clearly demonstrates that when attempts are made to control at a human level what is in reality an expression of the evolutionary force, the problems invariably continue to get worse as long as there is conscious or sub-conscious resistance to them. For it appears that the purpose of these apparent difficulties is to alert the individual to the fact that it is one's own misconception of one's needs that is the very thing which prevents one from having them fulfilled, and that once this is recognised and relinquished the creative principle is able to manifest at both an inner and an outer level and apparent miracles occur.

## Backache *or back pains*

These are often of sudden and unexpected onset, as in the case of headaches, and can be experienced as a sharp pain which is localised, or may be felt as a dull ache that can sometimes increase in intensity causing the perception of the pain to be referred out, so that it seems to come from other parts of the body in the immediate region. But whether this stress is experienced in the spinal column or in peripheral parts of the body, or even at some more subtle level of the psyche, these various manifestations are not mutually exclusive and the end result is always to advance the evolutionary process. Referring to this aspect Dr Sannella quotes Hans Selye as defining this stress as 'a state manifested by a specific syndrome which consists of all the nonspecifically induced changes within a biological system'. He enlarges on this observation by adding:

> The intensity of the symptoms is an index of the severity of the stress being released. . . . The unusual aspect of this mechanism is that the release of stress is experienced as a localised stimulation of a particular part of the body, as opposed to the accepted notion that stress is a diffuse general state.

What follows are a few examples of the kind of statement made in this regard:

> I have been having this feeling of heat in the lower back which comes and goes.

> Often when I go to bed at night I get cramp and tingling in my legs which gradually moves up to my back.

> I get these vibrations in my back which feels like energy pulsating. It is always accompanied by feelings of being supercharged and also by an increase in my sex drive.

One woman who had an unusually severe backache of sudden onset said:

> I felt very tired . . . then experienced a very severe pain in the

back. Pain spread through every part of my body. I then passed onto another dimension and was conscious of the most wonderful golden light. Feelings of absolute peace and bliss flooded over me.

In common with headaches, these backaches usually stop when the individual no longer resists the process (usually due to fear of the unknown). Once they understand what is happening to them, that the process is essentially one of purification and balancing, they learn to 'go with the flow' and the symptoms disappear.

### Itching, tingling or vibrating

Sometimes individuals going through the process may complain of itching, tingling or other sensations, which can either be on the surface of the skin or can be felt deep inside. These sensations can be experienced anywhere in the body, but a typical kundalini cycle will start in the feet, moving up the legs and back and ending in the head. It then descends down over the forehead, face and throat, finally coming to rest in the solar plexus. But this ordered progression is rarely encountered and more people report some, but seldom all, the manifestations. Those mentioned are quoted below:

For some time now I have been bothered by itching and a rash which comes and goes. It is always accompanied by waves of heat that engulf my entire body. There does not seem to be any medical explanation for it and it has been put down to an undetermined allergic reaction.

I also find that since my experience I have become sensitive to many things that didn't bother me before. I seem to have developed allergic reactions, especially to drugs and allopathic medicine, also to synthetic materials.

As well as the hot flashes, I seem at times to have a great concentration of heat in the area of my genitals . . . one day I felt something at the edge of my anus and was surprised to discover a large blister which I can only imagine must have been caused by the heat generated in that area.

The only physical sensation I am aware of now that I don't remember having before is a strange itching sensation inside the legs. I cannot relieve it by scratching the skin as it's deep inside my legs.

As well as all the other symptoms mentioned in this chapter these may well be due to some cause not generally recognised by the medical profession as a whole. Referring to this problem, Dr Sannella has observed:

It should now be clear that physicians are well advised to be alert for symptom patterns suggestive of kundalini arising. . . . In addition to psychotherapy, if indicated, we recommend that persons suspected of kundalini problems be urged to see someone with kundalini experience, as well.

### Fluctuations in body temperature and energy levels

Extremes of heat and cold are common manifestations of this phenomenon. They can be experienced in a specific area of the body or can be diffused throughout the whole system, in which case the heat is felt to spread throughout the individual to all parts of the body. Attempting to describe this sensation is usually regarded as difficult, but the accounts portrayed below give some idea of the feelings involved:

If I wasn't a man I would think I was going through the change of life, which in a sense I suppose I am. I get this strange feeling of heat flooding through me which I can only describe as being like an account of 'hot flushes'.

I get alternations of intense heat and intense cold. These feelings come on very suddenly and usually last for a few minutes, after which time my body temperature returns to normal. I feel this is associated with a new awareness and that somehow my body acts like an internal thermostat which registers external conditions.

Great heat in my legs, especially in the left leg, but on feeling them, expecting them to be very hot, they do not seem to be any different from normal.

At times my hands seem to radiate heat which can be quite clearly felt by others who have often remarked upon the fact.

An extended example of this aspect which on this occasion went to another extreme, in that unusual coldness was generated, was reported by a woman who felt that her NDE had activated a process of transformation that included a biological metamorphosis, during which time she underwent an experience similar to that of hibernation. This seems to have been a less extreme form of the suspended animation that is known to occur on occasions as a result of the chemical reactions that take place in the body during this process. She said of her experience:

After recovery from my near-death crisis I went through a very strange period of convalescence which at first I put down to being the after-effects of my illness. I became very cold and my temperature was discovered to be subnormal. It was also found that my pulse rate was abnormally slow and at the same time my blood pressure was alarmingly low. I felt unnaturally tired and looked white with dark circles under my eyes. I had no appetite and just wanted to sleep all the time. This condition became so acute that at one stage I was sent to hospital for two weeks and put under observation, during which time I underwent a number of tests. But the result of all this was that nothing organically wrong could be found and I was sent home still suffering from the same malady. During this time I was aware of an intense inner process taking place and the feeling I had at this time was similar to the tunnel experience. I felt as if I was in a dark 'womb'-like place and was about to be reborn. I could see light at the end of the passage, but I knew instinctively there was no way I could hurry the process and that it would come to an end in the fullness of time and I would emerge into the light reborn. The experience lasted about nine months, after which time the sensations abruptly ended and I felt totally different. It's almost impossible to describe because everything was the same as before and yet nothing was the same.

A related phenomenon is fluctuations of energy levels which, like those of body temperature, come and go without apparent explanation. The kind of sensations felt can be seen from the two descriptions given below:

> Another thing that has happened is that I get these sudden changes in energy. I can be feeling O.K. when – 'boom' – for no reason at all my energy level drops and I feel utterly exhausted. It's as if somebody had emptied all the stuffing out of a rag doll which is left limp and lifeless. That's how it feels. I feel my brain is affected at the same time. I feel disorientated and my brain feels fuzzy. On other occasions I feel supercharged, as if I had been plugged into a dynamo. I'm on a real 'high'. I have very strong sexual urges at this time and find sleep difficult. These feelings stop as suddenly as they started.

> For sometime now I have noticed that every now and then I am overcome with a most peculiar sort of tiredness. It comes on just like that [snaps her fingers]. I feel as if I am dying and that my life force is down to a tiny flicker, just a small puff would extinguish me. I recover from these strange bouts just as suddenly as it hits me. At other times I feel so charged up it's as if I can't contain any more energy or I will burn out at any minute. I'm not frightened by these experiences as I understand that it's necessarily a part of the transformation that I feel I am going through. Also I find it's better when I go along with these feelings and don't try to ignore them.

Although the kundalini process may make life difficult at times for those affected by its transforming physical and psychological influence, the disruptive element is greatly reduced when the anxieties surrounding these manifestations are explained in an atmosphere of understanding support. Without this help many people's physical burdens are increased by needlessly having to suffer mental affliction as well.

### Sensations of bodily expansion or contraction

This is somewhat different to out-of-the-body experiences where people view their surroundings from the location in which they find their psychical bodies. In this case, while individuals may get an elevated view of their surroundings, their perspective is nevertheless limited to the extent of their bodily expansion. As out-of-body experiences (OBEs) have been thoroughly investigated by a number of researchers, I do not propose to digress to a discourse on the subject, but will rather confine myself to quoting details of the relevant aspects only in this secton. The first deals with a simple sensation of bodily expansion and goes on to describe more extended versions of the same impressions:

> I sometimes get a strange feeling, it's very hard to describe, but my limbs feel enormous. It's as if I had blown up like a balloon . . . sort of round. I don't remember having these feelings before.

> It happened after I had been trying to release myself from my physical body so as to be less 'earth bound'. I suddenly felt my legs shoot out of their physical counterparts like a cork; they were at least ten inches longer. Then the same thing happened with my head, only a bit more slowly. I found that I had gone right through the wall at the back of my head and was looking at the other side of it. I particularly noticed a damp stain on the wall which was an odd shape. Later I got into the other room which was in neighbour's flat and asked if he would mind pulling the chest of drawers away from the wall that backed on to mine, as I wanted to examine the wall. And there was the stain just as I had seen it.

> I had been meditating quite intently and afterwards went for a stroll into the village to post a letter. Suddenly, without warning, I found myself extended in length so that my head was level with the tops of the trees on either side of the lane. It was a most extraordinary feeling. I remember feeling very 'spaced out' and strange. I got a sort of bird's eye view from up there . . . quite a different perspective. I turned slowly round and walked back home. I sat down under a tree with my back to the trunk and tried to ground myself. In a little while I felt back to normal size. This has not happened again, but I will never forget it; it was the most extraordinary sensation.

It seems that once an individual has experienced an OBE for whatever reason they are somehow less firmly rooted in physical matter and these experiences, along with all the other supernatural events described, are much more likely to be easily accomplished, either by an effort of will or spontaneously.

## Unusual perceptions of light or sound

Perceptions of light are one of the most noticeable features associated with the awakening of higher consciousness. It seems that when a very heightened state of illumination occurs at the level of understanding, it can also be reflected out and seems to be radiating from the 'enlightened' one. We all have an electromagnetic force field surrounding us, but it is generally invisible, firstly because most people's auras are very dull, and secondly because few people are able to see these emanations who do not possess the psychic gift of second sight. The most striking examples of light are those that have already been described in association with the NDE itself and are almost identical to those describing mystical experience; they usually seem to have the effect of alerting individuals to their inherent spiritual potential. A number of lights may appear subsequently to the brilliant one experienced during the NDE, but these usually take the form of lights which are 'seen' internally and which light up specific areas of the body such as the spine or head.

A man referred to me for help was suffering from a number of symptoms after an experience when he was suddenly hit by a bolt of light which bowled him over and temporarily blinded him. Following this incident he spontaneously developed the ability to be able to 'see' future events. Several times during the Falklands war he telephoned me to say he had 'seen' events taking place which were subsequently confirmed on television a few days later. Unfortunately he became somewhat unstable indulging in flights of fancy and self-aggrandisement. Not only have repeated warnings been made in the esoteric literature of the world that deals with the subject about the dangers inherent in falsely claiming this force to be an emanation of one's own ability, but, almost half a century ago, Jung, who was extremely interested in the kundalini phenomenon, observed that it was at one's peril that one claimed this force as one's own ego-creation. In almost all cases where the individuals concerned displayed psychotic tendencies, an inclination to ego inflation and false superiority were observed. This propensity was entirely absent in cases where transcendental elements were initiated by an NDE. The only cases I came across where psychotic manifestations were evident were in people who had endeavoured to activate this force prematurely without first having attended to their moral and spiritual development. Gopi Krishna also warns of the dangers attending this practice when there is 'morbid functioning of the evolution-ary mechanism', and speaking from his own experience describes how the activation of kundalini led him to near insanity and illness to the point of death.

Sounds are another manifestation that often accompanies the awakening of this dormant force. They include voices which are heard internally and can on occasions even be heard externally. Mostly these seem to come from the individuals' guides or can sometimes be recognised as the voice of a deceased loved one. A number of individuals felt these communications came from their own higher self. The content of these messages has already been examined both with regard to PFFs and PVs and also in those cases where information was given to people about healing techniques. I have come across a number of cases where false information was reported, but this did not happen in cases where the communication resulted from an NDE. Rather it almost always seemed to occur to people who had been dabbling in the occult: another very dangerous practice and one that can also lead on to manifestations of psychosis. There are occasions when a number of noises recognised as being characteristic of kundalini phenomena are heard; these can include roaring, whistling, hissing and sometimes bird-song or heavenly music.

The effects described so far range from objective manifestations to subjective sensations, but all point to a process in which the biological structure of the body's vital currents are slowly being modified. In the next category I will explore areas that concern the interpretation of the emotional and cognitive states that usually predominate at this time.

## Detachment or disassociation

This is a state wherein individuals typically feel detached from their experience and perceive themselves as witnessing all that is happening (including their thoughts and emotions) from a distance. Alluding to this state Dr Sannella remarks: 'It differs from aloofness or anxious withdrawal in that it is a disassociation of the separate observer-self from the mental activities that it observes. . . . Thus, this condition need not interfere with normal functioning.'

While this is going on there may be some distortions of cognitive process. Thoughts may appear to be speeded up or slowed down and an individual may experience being in a kind of limbo state of timelessness. Feelings of disorientation are also often present at this time. When this condition of withdrawal of self from identification with the ego and the gross physical world of matter is attained, the psyche begins to understand the truth of its being and starts to be free. But when it is unbalanced, due to fear and ignorance, there may be deep psychological resistances in which the negative aspects of the experience will become predominant. Once again Dr Sannella sums up the situation when he suggests that, in these circumstances,

> Hysteria or a state akin to schizophrenia may result. Also, the person may become identified with the physio-kundalini process itself in a negative, egotistical way, believing he or she has been divinely chosen for some great mission, perhaps as a saviour.

These initial stages of imbalance can be overcome in time with firm handling and understanding support. Given the right environmental assistance and an outgoing focus for these energies, in most cases, if not all, the negative manifestations gradually disappear.

With the exception of the non-physiological aspects of kundalini that include OBEs and psychic perception, which have already been described elsewhere in this book, this completes the survey of the components which Dr Sannella identifies as kundalini manifestations. Altogether, the material from his investigation, and the corroborative evidence of my own observations dealing with this phenomenon, combine to produce a fairly clear image of this system of human evolution. Neither the manifestations themselves nor their underlying dynamics are particularly puzzling, nor unduly problematical, once they are accepted and the reason for their appearance understood.

It would seem that similar physiological mechanisms are operating in both the NDE and kundalini phenomena and that they are both aspects of the same evolutionary force. Taken together, these spectacular instances of transformation add up to a surprisingly large and increasing percentage of the population and might therefore be expected to have a growing influence on the collective awareness of the rest of the species, at both a conscious and a subconscious level. We know that we have to grow and evolve, and that when this process is arrested or obstructed it leads to pathological states. An example is that of the suspected link between growth that has been stunted and cancer. It is as if the organism, prevented from developing to its full potential, turns in upon itself and grows in an unnatural or morbid way.

One only has to look around one to see that we are today witnessing the death of an old world and the birth of a new. Many of the psychological states that attend dying, which have been identified by Elisabeth Kübler-Ross, apply to life conditions as the world itself faces a near-death crisis. But at the same time it would appear that a new breed of mankind may be about to be born, and that in order for this to happen our consciousness and biological structure is undergoing a radical transformation. What we seem to be observing is a rebirth process which, when enabled to progress to completion, will eventually culminate in bringing forth an enlightened human being who has knowledge of the life and order of the universe.

The incidents described in this book, and the changes that have been wrought by their influence, point to the probability that the experiencers of these events are the forerunners of this new species. Referring to this metamorphosis in his book *Cosmic Consciousness*, Richard Bucke, a Canadian physician who made a study at the turn of the century of people who had attained this elevated state, writes: 'Along with the consciousness of the cosmos there occurs an intellectual enlightenment or illumination which alone would place the individual on a new plane of existence – would make him almost a member of a new species.' This, taken together with the physiological changes that have been noted, would lead one to surmise that this must have been what St John the Divine saw in his vision, that it was knowledge of this transformative event that prompted him to prophesy: 'And I saw a new heaven and a new earth, for the first heaven and the first earth were passed away, and there was no more sea.' For, when we are consciously living in harmony with cosmic consciousness, we will neither genetically inherit subconscious blocks to our progress, nor will we be creating additional subconscious problems, but as 'fully realised' beings will be able to live continually in communion with the Divine.

# CHAPTER 11
## *Explanations and interpretations of near-death experiences*

For now we see through a glass darkly.
*Corinthians*

The point has now been reached where, having presented the evidence that as far as I am able to determine seems to be associated with the NDE, I am faced with the task of attempting to interpret these findings. So I will try to do this in the first place by taking a look at some of the current theories that have been put forward by other researchers, and also examine a number of the interpretations propounded by the detractors of the NDE as well, in order to see if they can provide a satisfactory solution to the mysteries surrounding death. I shall start by considering those interpretations that relate to the NDE itself and then go on to examine some of the explanations that might account for phenomena associated with the after-effects.

Obviously, a number of explanations exist which have been proposed by scientifically minded people who feel that the kind of research that has been carried out to date still leaves many unresolved issues, since scientific methods are simply not available at this time to probe deeper. This leaves many individuals dissatisfied with the research that has been done in this field, largely because of the inherent limitations of such research. So, in order to try to come a little closer to an understanding of the near-death encounter, I propose to examine some of the naturalistic explanations that have been put forward to account for NDEs as a whole, so as to see if they can provide us with any answers.

Among the potentially relevant possibilities that exist are those that propose a dynamic interpretation such as depersonalisation and wishful thinking. Other explanations put forward to account for the NDE include pharmacological, physiological and neurological factors. Finally there are those who say that it can be explained away on the grounds of religious interpretations. But the problem here is that it is not possible to *prove* these theories; the naturalistic explanations are in fact just as speculative as the religious ones, for the experience itself is beyond the reach of scientific testability. Nevertheless, just because there is a limit to the possibilities of scientific methodology does not mean that NDEs should be written off as being unworthy of serious consideration.

So let us first consider whether the explanations and interpretations outlined here can provide us with a satisfactory reason to account for NDEs, for only if these proposals are unconvincing are we justified in moving on to a consideration of the alternative possibilities. In the light of this argument let us therefore see what these possible solutions will disclose.

## PSYCHOLOGICAL INTERPRETATIONS

### Depersonalisation

Among the psychological interpretations, the theory of depersonalisation has been put forward as a likely answer to explain reactions to perception of impending death. Noyes and Kletti have been foremost in advancing the psychodynamic explanation for this possibility. This is a psychological condition that is understood as an ego-defence mechanism, which allows individuals to protect themselves from the unacceptable realities of impending death. Despite the fact that this would seem on the surface to be a fairly plausible explanation, a number of inconsistencies argue its rejection. In the first place, the classic descriptions of depersonalisation, which include a feeling of unreality, differ in many ways from the psychological state of the near-death survivor. And secondly, the psychological detachment of depersonalisation is very different from the feeling of total reality which many respondents emphasise while 'out of their body'.

Furthermore, depersonalisation is unable to account for those cases of NDE wherein a deceased relative, whose demise the dying individual had no prior knowledge of, is encountered and communicated with. Apart from the cases already alluded to (which included the woman in hospital suffering from heart disease, who heard of her aunt's death from her already deceased mother with whom she met and conversed during the time she was clinically dead, the aunt's death being later confirmed by relatives visiting the hospital), perception of a deceased relative, by a dying individual who did not know that the relative in question was dead, has also been noted by Kenneth Ring and Elisabeth Kübler-Ross, who have recounted episodes of this kind.

While stress is undoubtedly able to trigger a defensive reaction to begin with, as Kenneth Ring points out in *Life at Death*, 'the transcendental realities that appear to an individual confronted with death may represent a higher dimension of consciousness and not just a symbolic fantasy rooted in denial'; and he goes on to say that instead of following the 'well known tendency of orthodox psychoanalysis towards facile reductionism, it might be more important to listen carefully to the testimony of near-death survivors than to follow the predilectons of Freud'. He concludes that the 'psychoanalytic attempt to explain away NDEs as depersonalisation seems both forced and inadequate'.

## Wishful thinking

This is another assumption which has been considered in the light of the possible desire to turn the apparent finality of death into death-defying feelings of bodily detachment and mystical transcendence, which include vistas of a heavenly after-life. This supposition has been rejected by both Raymond Moody and Kenneth Ring on the grounds that, as with the depersonalisation interpretation, this position does not stand up to scrutiny for the same reason that it too fails to explain cases where a deceased relative whose death was unknown to the near-death survivor was reported to have been seen.

Neither can it explain other factors that are incompatible with the wishful thinking hypothesis. For example, Kenneth Ring has pointed out that it is unable to account for 'the *consistent patterning* of the core experience across different people' because, as he says, this in itself is 'evidence against the hypothesis'. He further adds:

> Presumably, people differ in their wishes in regard to a hoped-for afterlife, yet the sequence of experiences they go through in coming close to death is remarkably alike. It is also noteworthy that the experiences of non-believers and suicide attempters also tend, on the whole, to conform to the general patterning of the core experience – yet one would imagine they would wish for the cessation of consciousness.

In other words, as he says, the 'wishful thinking explanation appears to be . . . wishful thinking!'

### Prior expectations

Another related aspect that has been investigated and found wanting is that of the individual's prior expectations. People tend to stress that their experiences were often very different from what they had been led to expect as a result of their religious indoctrination, and have said that they were often surprised to find that what they actually encountered was decidedly different from the conventional representations of heaven or hell. It therefore seems improbable, from the experiences related, that religious-based expectations shape NDEs. For, whether people are religiously minded or religiously indifferent, the likelihood of their having an NDE proves to be the same, the only difference being the influence religion has on their interpretation of the experience.

Finally, if prior expectations were conducive to the construction of NDEs, one would suppose that those already familiar with this experience at the time of their own near-death episode would be more likely to report such experiences. Instead the *reverse* occurs; for, as Kenneth Ring discovered (and my research has endorsed), uninformed respondents describe proportionately more NDEs. Thus, the effort to explain the NDE in terms of such psychological concepts as depersonalisation, wishful thinking or prior expectations has proved ineffectual. Other explanations will therefore have to be explored.

## Psychoanalytic interpretations

This book is not the place to discuss in any detail the merits or otherwise of the great analytical systems of psychology, for as Anita Gregory, who is one of the foremost psychical researchers in this country, pointed out to me in a personal communication:

> Taken as overall doctrines they may be used, or perhaps unused, to prove or disprove anything: it is precisely this invulnerability to disproof which is often seen, from a scientific point of view, as constituting a considerable weakness. On the other hand, such systems have shed much light on obscure corners of the human condition.

It might, however, seem desirable to look at some of the more obvious possible piecemeal interpretations of this type that have been suggested, and these are briefly discussed in the section headed Paranormal developments.

# PHARMACOLOGICAL AND PHYSIOLOGICAL CONSIDERATIONS

## Anaesthetics

It has been observed by other researchers (notably Raymond Moody who was the first to draw attention to this fact) that occasionally the use of anaesthetics is associated with phenomena that bear some similarity to NDEs. Whether drugs are ingested medically or taken illegally they can on occasions induce a euphoric 'high' or cause a 'bad trip'. involving terrifying distortions of perception. This being the case, could anaesthetics alone trigger an NDE, independent of the near-death state? In theory it would be possible if the administration of anaesthetics produced a raising of carbon dioxide, a condition known to cause visionary type experiences. While allowing for variations in anaesthetics, properly administered, however, they have no specific effect on the carbon dioxide levels and, in cases of cardiac arrest during surgery, the anaesthetic is in fact shut off and the patient is given oxygen instead. But there is also some evidence that anaesthetics may even interfere with the occurrence of NDEs, as anaesthetised patients typically tend not to have recall of any kind afterwards. Moreover, if some experience is described, the experience more often than not deviates in obvious ways from the typical NDE pattern and is more likely to resemble a hallucination. Dr Sabom, referring to this fact in *Recollections of Death,* writes: 'Medical studies of the content and structure of drug-induced hallucinations have found these experiences to be highly variable and idiosyncratic', showing that drug-induced delusions are markedly different from NDEs, which always show a remarkable degree of invariance. Lastly, a number of respondents who described an NDE never received any anaesthetics at all or even any medical treatment. Thus, if the effect can at times be observed in the absence of the reputed cause, obviously that hypothesis is an erroneous one. Therefore, the conclusion must be that even though anaesthetics may not preclude phenomena associated with near-death experiences, such experiences cannot be explained by them.

*Cerebral anoxia*

The most frequently suggested physiological explanation for NDEs offers insufficient oxygen as a likely cause. In view of the physiological deterioration that sets in as death approaches, revealing itself in such conditions as decreased blood pressure and cardiac and respiratory failure, which would tend to bring about this precise effect, it would seem reasonable to suppose that the depleted physiological state of the individual would somehow trigger an NDE. At first glance this would seem to be a reasonable theory when one considers the fact that the great majority of NDErs are unconscious at the time of their experience. However, it seems extremely unlikely that everyone of these people would have experienced significant anoxia to account for the phenomenon; moreover, this supposition is in direct opposition to what appears to be the causative factor in hyperventilation related NDEs, where, of course, patients suffer from an excess of oxygen.

Finally, even if more proof were needed to cast doubt on the cerebral anoxia hypothesis, the fact remains that visionary aspects of the NDE were often found in conscious patients whose experience occurred well before the final descent into the coma that typically precedes death. It is therefore difficult to interpret the phenomenon from the standpoint of cerebral anoxia.

## Neurological factors

One of the biochemical mechanisms that has been suggested to account for NDEs is temporal lobe seizure. Although some similarities do exist between experiences induced by temporal lobe stimulation or those associated with temporal lobe seizures on the one hand and an NDE on the other, many differences between the two are also apparent. Raymond Moody, Kenneth Ring and Michael Sabom have all considered this as a possibility and have come to the conclusion that this mechanism is inadequate to explain the complete range of near-death phenomena. Furthermore, a number of significant differences have been observed to occur in temporal lobe seizures that set them apart from NDEs, notably perception of the immediate environment is often distorted, which is in complete contrast to that reported in NDEs. It therefore seems that the evidence to date rules out any neurological interpretations that attempt to link the NDE with temporal lobe seizures.

This brief summary has covered, in general terms, what appears to be the status of the proposed psychological, pharmacological and physiological explanations. Research to date has rendered them unlikely, but obviously much more research would need to be done in this area before any definite conclusions could be reached. However, as Kenneth Ring has observed, 'Simply because no one has yet found the neurological key to unlock the mysteries of the near-death experience doesn't mean that none exists.' Nevertheless, now that the NDE has been identified as a feature of the dying process, it is to be hoped that continued research and debate in this field will reveal as yet undiscovered aspects relating to the phenomenon. Again, with regard to future research, Dr Ring has cautioned potential investigators that any naturalistic interpretation would need to show how the *entire complex* of phenomena that is associated with NDEs could be accommodated within a specific explanation. As he says:

It is not difficult – in fact it is easy – to propose naturalistic interpretations that could conceivably explain some aspect of the core experience. Such explanations, however, sometimes seem merely glib and are usually of the 'this-is-nothing-but-an-instance-of' variety; rarely do they seem to be seriously considered attempts to come to grips with a very puzzling phenomenon. . . . Indeed, I am tempted to argue that the burden of proof has now shifted to those who wish to explain near-death experiences in this way.

Meanwhile, all we can do is to keep an open mind on this question, while awaiting more conclusive interpretations of the physiological roles to be explained.

## PARANORMAL DEVELOPMENTS

This brings me to a consideration of some of the phenomena that have been discussed in association with the after-effects. In seeking to understand these paranormal developments, it must be decided how to evaluate these claims. In the first place, the question is – is it possible to have a paranormal knowledge of future events, and in the second are these 'flash forwards' actually prophetic visions, or can they be explained in another way?

The foremost question then to be resolved is one of precognition. Although there are a number of theories as to what happens in an altered state of consciousness regarding the apparent ability to be able to transcend time and space while in this condition, so far there has been no general agreement on this point. Mystics have alluded to these theories for hundreds of years, but it was only towards the end of the last century that parapsychologists started seriously to investigate a subject that has recently come to be the focus of considerable attention by scientists also. For what now appears to be emerging is the discovery that new phenomena may in reality be true anomalies which our previous beliefs were unable to accommodate.

Taken at a phenomenological level undoubtedly a total collapse of one's linear time sense seems to occur in altered states of consciousness and this is particularly common in NDEs. But, even if we accept that in this state precognition is possible and visionary knowledge of future events can occur, there still remain a number of alternative interpretations, and unless reasons can be found that necessitate rejection of them, there is no obligation to accept these apocalyptic pronouncements as being of any particular significance for future world conditions. For, as Kenneth Ring has pointed out, the interpretation of prophetic visions 'needs to be made with utmost caution, particularly given their extreme content and their capacity, if taken seriously, to generate a wide range of individual and collective reactions based on fear, hysteria, or simply passivity'. He has therefore proposed a number of 'possible interpretations' to explain this phenomenon, so, taking this as the basis for a parallel examination, I now intend to evaluate his propositions.

### Psychodynamic interpretation of prophetic visions

The first possibility to be considered is whether these visions might be psychodynamic in origin. This is a process whereby people project their own fears (which may be unconscious) onto something outside of themselves. In the case of calamitous prophetic visions it is easy to see how this could apply, when one considers that during a near-death crisis an individual's fear of extinction could become externalised onto a supposedly doomed location. Another version of this kind of possibility has been suggested by Kenneth Ring, whereby an individual who is, after all, very close to death at the time could have 'unconsciously registered the physical symptoms of [his or her] near-death state and [have] used them as an inadvertent basis on which to generalise. . . . "the death of the world". That is, since he is dying, he somehow transfers this into "the world is dying".'

Although at first glance this might seem to be a possibility, these psychodynamic constructions do not really stand up to scrutiny. For instance, the similarity of content makes this interpretation unlikely: as Dr Ring points out, 'Why not a greater variety of projected global futures since near-death survivors can be expected, like the rest of us, to have a considerable range of expectations of the future?' But this is not the case, as they all have a recurrent theme. Furthermore, if the scenario presented a projection of their own unconscious conflicts, why is the overwhelming overall feeling that accompanies these near-death encounters so positive? One might expect the reverse to be the case if prophetic visions were in fact a generalised projection of the individual's expected demise.

It would therefore seem that without a great many extra complexities a psychodynamic attempt to explain prophetic visions is not an adequate one.

## Archetypal interpretations

This is another interpretation that has been suggested to account for the visionary aspects of NDEs. Here the prophetic vision is seen as a 'reflection of the universal death-rebirth motif' that is found in mythology and religion and, furthermore, can be experienced directly in certain profound altered states of consciousness. This is known to occur in some acute psychotic states as well and has also been noted in research with psychedelic drugs which have disclosed death-rebirth archetypes. I am inclined to feel that a more generalised archetypal interpretation is a possibility in cases of hell-like experiences, where negative emotions which have become trapped in the psyche are released during a near-death episode. While this may be an explanation for hellish type experiences, it seems inadequate to account for prophetic visions, with their occasional paranormal and veridical content, which would seem to require a transpersonal or superconscious rather than a primitive archetypal interpretation. The following quotation, which comes from a woman whose NDE resulted from a car accident, illustrates this point:

> I was driving back from London to Luxembourg, where I was working with the European Parliament, when about midnight I hit a patch of black ice going round a curve on the edge of a ravine and went into a skid. My left rear tyre hit a low barrier separating the two lanes of traffic which caused the tyre to burst. The car turned over and the last thing I remember is feeling ice on my face. I next found myself spiralling out of my body, rushing back over the route I had come. I noticed back around the bend in the road an oncoming car with an elderly couple inside. The man lifted

his hands off the wheel when he heard the crash, at the same time the pipe he was smoking dropped into his lap. He turned to his wife and said, 'Here we go, *again*.' I saw him trying to brush the cinders from the fallen pipe off his trousers. I then felt myself being drawn up a dark tube or funnel. I could see a radiance at the top and there was a vague impression of a figure who offered me a beautiful shawl, all white and soft and luminous. I heard him say, 'Come, you must be so cold, so tired.' I rather got an impression of this communication as I don't remember any words being spoken. I was aware of people all around me, but I couldn't actually see anyone. Next, I heard a friend who had died about seven or eight years before saying, 'It's not meant. He didn't really mean it, it's not meant.' On this occasion I quite clearly heard her voice; it was not a mental communication as it was with the figure of light. I had felt an impulse to go forward, to accept the shawl and to be enveloped by its cosy warmth. But her voice somehow prevented me from going forward, and I stopped to think. I remember saying, 'No, I'm sorry, I can't accept your lovely shawl as I'm all covered in blood.' I looked down and could see myself inside the car covered in blood. I don't remember how I returned. The next thing that happened was I regained consciousness. Everyone was amazed for they were convinced I was dead. I too feel I died. . . . The next morning I said to the man, 'When you heard the accident, why did you say "again"?' He said, 'I don't understand.' So I said, 'You turned to Madame and at the same time dropped your pipe out of your mouth.' He turned extremely white and said, 'But Madame, you couldn't possibly know that because you were in the crash round the corner.' I feel I was gone and made the choice to come back.

## MISCELLANEOUS CONSIDERATIONS

### Zeitgeist interpretation

As we move towards the end of the millenium there looms the

threat of widespread death and destruction, not only through the possibility of nuclear war, but as a result of the constant wars going on around the world, riots, rising crime, vandalism, racial disorders and severe sociological upheavals of all kinds. As people's fear and confusion increase they seek for answers to their dilemma and try to satisfy their doubts by finding explanations for the current state of affairs. Many current interpretations of the Bible, as well as a number of popular books, are suggesting that we are fast approaching the apocalyptic age. When we add to this a number of well-documented instances of religious apparitions, such as the so-called Fatima miracle, where the 'Heavenly Mother' appeared to three small children and gave revelations of coming world events that could only be avoided if people changed their ways in time, it can be readily understood that many people are likely to be influenced. However, as Dr Ring suggests, since 'All these fears and expectations . . . have been "in the air" for some time, is it not possible that near-death survivors are simply "picking up on" what many people think and feel? If this were the case then no special signficance need be given to these visions.

But there are two considerations that have to be borne in mind when evaluating this interpretation. First, there is no such thing as time (as we understand it) on the 'other side', and it is well known that predictions are notoriously difficult to date correctly. This has led to the axiom that 'it is the destiny of prophets to make themselves look foolish'. The second point that has to be considered is that even if and when the predicted event does take place, it is often far from as bad as envisaged. Given that certain occurrences do sometimes happen as indicated, albeit to a lesser extent, these incidents should 'give us pause that even a collectively shared vision such as a PV must have predictive significance'. This being the case, the *Zeitgeist* theory is the one most likely to have a bearing on the content of PVs.

There still remains the interpretation that most of the individuals who have had a PV are inclined to put on their experience, and that is the prophetic one. A number of near-death survivors did in fact feel they had been 'singled out' to receive this information so as to be able to alert others to the urgent need to change things.

There is of course no way (as the major events predicted have not yet taken place) that this interpretation can be verified so far.

But there is another possibility that is known as the 'alternative future interpretation', whereby only probabilities are regarded as predictable. This implies that PVs represent only one of several alternative futures and that what is predicted is but one of the possibilities. It has been reported by near-death experiencers that, during the expansion of consciousness that can take place while out of the body, they sometimes become aware of several 'lines of trajectories that would lead towards futures'. One line concerns events that would have developed if the course of history had been different, another the classic PV scenario and a third involves an even more destructive version of the events that have so far been envisaged.

The conclusion is therefore that these PVs may represent only one of a number of future scenarios and that the individuals concerned, not realising that there might be another possibility, took their alternative future for the *only* future. So that while they feel certain they have experienced the shape of things to come, it may not necessarily be the right one. Of course, even if the alternative futures interpretation outlined here is correct, one would still have to ask: why are reports of PVs seemingly limited to the one future herein described?

Before concluding this chapter in which I have examined some of the explanations and interpretations offered by other researchers, but more especially by Kenneth Ring, I want to raise a few issues that pertain to an evaluation of the other paranormal developments. That is, how is it possible to know if the ability to effect apparently miraculous cures is authentic, or are there in fact some other factors that may account for the seemingly impossible event?

*Hypnosis*

One of the possibilities put forward to account for this paranormal ability is hypnosis or suggestion. It has been proposed, for instance, that the apparent miracles discussed in the chapter on healing manifestations are merely an instance of induced mesmerism, whereby people seeking help are so desperate that they are in the right frame of mind to be conditioned to respond to any external ideas that will bring about a cure. Another version of this kind of interpretation is that of auto-suggestion. In this case the idea that healing is possible is introduced to the thoughts of the individuals seeking help, who are then so convinced they will recover that in many instances they do.

Although superficially plausible, these interpretations fail in certain respects. For instance, they cannot account for those occasions where the individual was unaware that he or she was being given healing (as in the case of the young girl whose mother interceded on her behalf). Furthermore, it is generally assumed that in order for subjects to be hypnotised they need to be in the presence of the hypnotist in the first instance, and this was clearly not the case in a number of examples. Hypnosis at a distance, which has been claimed and reasonably well established, notably by the Russian physiologist L. L. Vasiliev, is of course another matter, and could hardly serve as a 'normal', or for that matter any other, explanation, and this is not the place to discuss this issue. I am, therefore, inclined to look elsewhere for an explanation of psychic healing.

### Spontaneous remission

Whenever a cure is effected for which there is no apparent explanation and which cannot be explained by physical intervention, one of the most convenient ways of accounting for this event is to dismiss it with the observation that it was obviously one of those cases of spontaneous remission. While cases of spontaneous remission do undoubtedly occur, there is almost always an extra dimension, an unacknowledged and sometimes unknown factor, which has played a decisive part in bringing this about. Writing about this occurrence in *Getting Well Again*, Carl and Stephanie Simonton argue:

> The number of spontaneous remissions from cancer appears to be small, though all estimates are guesses because we have no idea how many such remissions take place before

patients are diagnosed as having the disease. Yet however many cases there are, none of them is 'spontaneous'. In each case there is some kind of cause-and-effect process. The process by which spontaneous remission takes place is simply beyond our present understanding.

It would appear from these considerations that the cures which have been effected by NDErs as a result of the healing ability which developed from their experience cannot be explained away on the grounds of spontaneous remission, other than that the intercession of the healer could be accounted as the unknown factor, and so another explanation will have to be sought.

### Faith healing

The final possibility I would like to consider is one which is often suggested to explain healing that cannot be accounted for by the usual methods: the element of belief. However, although faith undoubtedly plays a part in making the individual who seeks healing more responsive to healing, faith alone, especially at a merely cognitive level, does not seem to be able to effect a cure: otherwise everyone who believed would be healed, which is clearly not the case. It is not the act, which often accompanies these healings, of 'laying on of hands' *per se* which produces the cure, but it is the ability of the healer to be able to contact a power or force that resides without and within, and which is not generally recognised or sought after unless contact has already been established. Thus the explanation proposed is of no more help than the others in seeking to understand the riddle of how this healing comes about.

In the meantime, I think it is fair to conclude that the interpretations so far suggested are not adequate to solve this enigma; the decisive explanation of this phenomenon has yet to be articulated. Now that the appearance of paranormal after-effects following NDEs has been established, it is to be hoped that other researchers will take up the challenge and continue to build on the work that has been started.

While awaiting a reasonable interpretation, it seems that other lines of inquiry may be more rewarding in offering an explanation of both the NDE itself and also of the paranormal developments associated with the after-effects. In the final chapter I will be concerned with exploring some of the more esoteric concepts that have been propounded to account for these seemingly impossible events in an effort to understand the mysteries surrounding them.

# CHAPTER 12
## *Reflections on some possible implications*

The last enemy that shall be destroyed is death.
*Corinthians*

I have now reached the final stage of my study where I am ready to inquire into the meaning and significance of the experience. I have shown what it is like to die and what apparently happens to those who have gone as far as it is possible to go. I have examined the effects of the experience on the lives of those people who returned from their near-death encounter and considered some of the theoretical explanations that have been proposed to account for the occurrence.

The evidence so far presented has shown that the event undoubtedly has a quality of subjective reality that is entirely authentic to the people who undergo it, which extends far beyond the limitations of sense perception. So what conceptual framework can best be utilised in order to understand the dynamics of the NDE? In my view, the perspective that offers the best possibility for attempting to understand the phenomenon is that provided by the mystical teachings.

There was a time when science was seen to be engaged in a life and death struggle with mysticism. However, in the past few decades it has become ever plainer that there is in fact no clash between physics and mysticism; many have gone further, and have even suggested that the language of the scientist and that of the mystic are converging. Be that as it may, it has become clear that science itself is only one path among others towards truth, and that, like other human activities, it undergoes change and transformation.

The idea that life continues after death varies of course with different cultures and ideologies, but basically what they are all saying is that death is not the end of existence, that in a different

186

form consciousness continues after the body is no longer vital. As Arthur Koestler, in writing about modern quantum physics in his book *The Roots of Coincidence*, has suggested, mystical experience is not nearly as mind-boggling as that of modern quantum physics, which even physicists sometimes confess to being unable to understand.

A mystical vision of the nature of the universe ultimately seems to offer the best basis for an understanding of NDEs. However, it is generally accepted by those who subscribe to this view that it will take a while before people begin to feel comfortable with an order of reality other than the world of appearances.

In the final analysis, science would seem to be converging with, or at least not conflicting with what mystics have asserted for millennia when they have stated that access to spiritual reality only becomes possible when consciousness is freed from its dependence on the physical body. So long as one remains tied to the body and its sensory perceptions, spiritual reality can at best never be more than an intellectual construct. For it is only when one approaches the realm beyond death that one can experience it directly.

Although the relevance of the possible neurological basis of the NDE is still a largely unexplored area, and while obviously research will continue to probe these matters ever more deeply for many years to come, the question of whether the mysteries of the NDE can ever be fully understood by 'scientific investigation' remains open to speculation. Current paradigm shifts would nevertheless seem to be leading to a recognition of the primary role of consciousness, in which the world of physics and the world of the spirit seem to reflect a single reality.

Before proceeding to the implications of the NDE and the transformation that often follows the experience, I want to point out that what have been presented are near-death phenomena, and that these are in no way intended to represent evidence of a life hereafter, as clearly not one of the respondents went further than surviving the initial stages of death. While I have found it necessary to take an objective line of approach in this work, I am conscious of the fact that in discussing the NDE with others I am invariably asked for my own views about life after death. This might therefore be an appropriate time to mention what I believe, for at this stage I feel confident that, in admitting that I am personally convinced we continue to have a conscious existence after physical death, I will not be unduly influencing readers who by now, I trust, will have had ample opportunity to arrive at some kind of assessment of their own. But just because I believe, as a result of my own experience and from my studies as a psychologist, that a near-death encounter is one of the ways we can become aware of other realities, it would be quite wrong to give the impression that my views are in any way intended as an endorsement of this assertion. I sincerely hope, though, that what has been presented here will have given readers an opportunity to make up their own minds about these issues, so as to reach an understanding of a concept that gives value and meaning to life.

What is evident is that many experience the 'luminosity', which, according to certain mystical traditions, arises out of that moment before death when one loses contact with the solid world which one experiences as dualistic. At that moment when consciousness dissolves into the 'sushumna nadi', which is described as the pathway of energy (prana) which is located in the spinal column of the body, there is a sense of internal luminosity.

This notion of ego-death and transcendence can also be found in other cultural traditions. Perhaps the earliest known records that give evidence of practices leading to transition from a state of consciousness rooted in our physical world of sensory impressions to one that is sensitive to the realities of another dimension of existence, are those relating to the temple sleep in ancient Egypt. The neophytes' training included being put into a state of suspended animation for three days and nights, during which time the spirit was said to leave the physical body, which remained in a death-like state, while it journeyed through other realms in order to learn certain lessons that were considered necessary for the spiritual development of the initiate. By this method consciousness is able to function independently of the physical body and becomes capable of awareness of another (fourth) dimension outside of the usual world of sensory reality.

These experiences share many phenomenological similarities with current sensory isolation practices, whereby the individual undergoing the experience very quickly loses all sense of reality due to a severe reduction of sensory-based input to the brain. When this happens, the individual may undergo what is known as an ego-death. For example, Stanislav Grof, a Czech psychoanalyst working in America, has proposed in his book *The Human Encounter with Death* that this process, (by which an individual 'dies to himself' in such a way that ordinary ego function is disrupted or absent), is a key transformative event in all mystical experience, whether induced or spontaneous. This is an intense emotional experience and while in this state there is a tremendous sense of encompassing oneness, in which an individual apparently invariably becomes aware of a higher transcendent order, which is always followed by feelings of rebirth and a certainty that consciousness is independent of the physical body and continues beyond physical death.

As has been noted previously, the elements encountered within the NDE are not unique to near-death episodes, but are potentially available to those who learn to operate their consciousness independently of the physical body. In the East, where religious philosophy is less restrictive, many spiritual disciplines are devoted to practices that attempt to trigger this release in order to induce such experiences. I have already referred to the underlying principle involved in the practice of kundalini yoga, which is probably the technique that has been most thoroughly studied by western scholars, but there are others. The practice of pranayama meditation is just such an example, which, according to Paramhansa Yogananda, if properly exercised can bring about precisely these effects by 'disjoining the course of inspiration and expiration' in order to switch the life current from the senses, so that the mind is withdrawn from the sensory world to the point where all sense of ego and separate identity disappear.

Another is associated with the opening of the so-called 'third eye'. This occurrence is also related to the development of higher states of consciousness and is regarded as a kundalini manifestation by Dr Sannella. Referring to this state, which he has termed 'single seeing', he says: 'Single seeing can be easily identified as a separate and distinct state by the typical and graphic metaphors used to describe the experience by people who have had it.' He quotes the case of a woman who said of this condition:

My sight had changed, sharpened to an infinitely small point which moved ceaselessly in paths totally free of the old accustomed ones, as if flowing from a new source.
It was as if some inner eye . . . which extended without

limit . . . had been restored . . . focused on infinity in a way that was detached from immediate sight and yet had a profound effect on sight . . . there was a sharp one-pointedness to my attention now rooted into some deeper centre so that my everyday sight, my eyes, were released from their [need] to see the world outside . . . no matter where I looked no shadow [image] of my nose . . . ever appeared in the clear field of sight.

Unfortunately in the West there is still only a rudimentary understanding of these manifestations and their association with certain physiological processes, and a tendency to include methods for attaining this state (whether spontaneously developed or deliberately induced) and the attending symptoms in the same category. But, according to certain Eastern teaching, this practice, which is known as Shiva Yoga, differs from Kundalini Yoga in a number of important ways. In the first place it is recognised that attempts to activate the kundalini force are often attended by difficulties and danger, as has already been shown, whereas the process of awakening the inner eye is regarded as simple and safe. This inner eye is considered to be connected with the pineal gland, and can either be galvanised into activity by certain yogi practices, or is spontaneously activated when the evolutionary force leaves the reproductive organs (as happens in near-death occurrences) to rush up the spinal column where it unites with forces residing in the brain.

Sri Kumarswamiji, an Indian yogi, little known outside his own country, who has made a life-long study of Shiva Yoga, has this to say on the subject of the pineal gland:

It represents all that remains of a third eye which used to adorn the forehead of some of the lizard ancestors in far off times. . . . The pineal gland is a rudimentary organ in most people but it is evolving though slowly. It is possible to quicken its evolution into a condition in which it can perform its function of apprehending events comprehensively and not piece-meal. The full development of this organ helps the Yogi to transcend mathematical time, which is only an illusion produced by the succession of states of consciousness, as one travels through eternal duration. In Yoga Shastra this pineal gland is sometimes spoken of as

> [the] third eye, the function of which takes place externally
> through the middle of the forehead. . . . This third eye is
> now atrophied, simply because the tendency of man has
> grown downward and has got immersed in sexual
> pleasures. . . . Scientists opine that the pineal gland is a relic
> of the third eye, hence it is vestigial. But the adepts affirm
> that it is embryonical and therefore it is capable of being
> developed.

From this account it is possible to see how the clairvoyant vision
experienced by some NDErs might possibly be accomplished.

Having reflected on some of the possible physiological
mechanisms implicated in near-death and mystical experiences, I
now want to move on to consider some of the psychological
processes that appear to be involved in certain states. The *Tibetan
Book of the Dead* is a manual of mystical teaching concerning the
nature of the mind and its projections that speaks to the living as
well as the dying. Included in its instructions is an account of
various *bardos* or psychological states of existence where
archetype images from the subconscious or lower realm entities
must be encountered and overcome before progress can be made.
My view is that this refers to 'unfinished business' that has become
trapped in the psyche or soul and which continues to cause
problems until recognised and overcome. When this occurs, the
emotional charge behind the event which has become blocked
energy can then be discharged and the passage to progress freed
from obstruction.

In cases of hell-like experience what seems to be happening is
that it is not the emotion that causes problems on the astral plane,
but rather the trouble is created as a result of what one chooses to
do with that emotion. This was well illustrated in the case of the
respondent who during her hell-like experience found herself
lying on the edge of the pit of hell, and who feared that a large lion
which she saw on the other side of the pit and which seemed about
to spring upon her would dislodge her and send her down into
that awful place. Her fear was not so much of the lion, which
symbolised her feelings of destructive rage, but what it might do to
her. When one considers the events that led up to her NDE, the
psychological form it took becomes more understandable. It
transpires that some time before her experience her husband had

gone off with a younger woman. She was feeling so enraged that she refused to give him a divorce and had instructed her solicitor to sue for maintenance so as to make things financially as difficult as possible for them. What makes her story so interesting is that she was not afraid of her anger, because anger is in reality neither good nor bad, it just is. But she was afraid of what her anger might do to her, for the expression of her anger was in danger of pushing her into the pit of hell.

I came across an account of a similar incident while I was visiting the ashram of Sri Aurobindo and the Mother, at Pondicherry in Southern India, which was experienced by a pupil of the Mother during an out-of-the-body episode. The encounter, with a tiger this time, was similar and also related to feelings of extreme anger directed towards someone who the subject felt had wronged him. The story concerned a young man who, along with a number of other advanced students of the Mother, underwent some kind of initiation experience. I am not certain what method was used to induce an altered state of consciousness, but I think it involved some sort of sensory deprivation. This particular pupil found himself 'out of his body' walking down a jungle path, when suddenly he was confronted by an enormous, ferocious tiger which looked as if it was about to spring on him and tear him limb from limb. He remembered the Mother's injunction that whatever transpired he was to stand his ground and show no fear, otherwise he would be overpowered by the manifestation and destroyed. So he confronted the tiger and he looked at it; it gradually shrank and shrank until it became a little domestic cat and walked off into the jungle. Upon relating this story to the Mother later, she appeared very interested and asked if shortly before undergoing the experience he had felt great enmity and rage for anyone. The young man replied that as a matter of fact he had indeed felt just such an emotion, for prior to the experience his wife had run off with his best friend and he had been aware that, if he could have got his hands on them, he would have liked to have 'torn them limb from limb'. The Mother retorted that it was just as she had supposed, for what he had faced were his own 'thought forms' or projections which had materialised and like a boomerang had turned upon him. But by confronting his rage and overcoming it he had tamed it; so that like a little domestic cat it had disappeared into the jungle without harming him. For so long as his anger was suppressed, he was unable to transcend it.

As these episodes have shown, the encounters with animals that are symbolic of destructive rage, which both these individuals were harbouring in their psyche at the time of their respective experiences, were similar and were directed towards people whom the relaters felt had wronged them.

What then are the inherent implications of the NDE and their relevance to personal psychology? The nature of reality is something that affects us all, and we must all ultimately deal with these larger issues, which form the underlying values of our lives and give them direction, if we are to develop beyond our present limitations. What happens in the realms beyond this stage of near-death does not concern us here. But what the NDE has shown us are ways in which we may progress and how our lives can be infinitely enlightened while we are still living on this human level of existence.

One of the fundamental principles arising out of all philosophies that are concerned with death and rebirth is that it is a situation which is recurring constantly in this life. In the *Tibetan Book of the Dead* it is the *bardo* or gap that is emphasised, which is not only the interval of suspension after we die, but also the suspension in the living condition and as such is part of our basic psychological make-up. Every time we find ourselves in a situation where we are unsure of our ground and feel ourselves to be losing contact with the solid world, the possibility exists of stepping out of the apparent world of reality into a world beyond that of the senses. That, in my view, is the reason why people who are having a psychotic episode, and also those facing a severe life-threatening situation, are both likely candidates for mystical experience.

The ever-increasing frequency of NDEs seems to be directly related to the evolutionary process of which many enlightened beings are becoming ever more aware, and it could be that higher consciousness is attempting to alert us on a collective level to the urgent need for a universal brotherhood, based on love and goodwill, manifesting in compassion. We thus seem to be moving away from an individualistic approach to one of collective co-operation based on self-responsibility. While the resistance to this is very strong, revealing itself in the increasing breakup of the old social order which created a dependent society that looked towards the welfare state, or alternatively sought a guru or father-figure to take responsibility and blame for individuals' lives, the need is emerging to realise that we are not victims of fate, both individually and collectively: 'Each man is his own absolute lawgiver, the dispenser of glory or gloom to himself, the decreer of his life, his reward, his punishment' (Mabel Collins, quoted by Ramacharaka). Do we have to wait until the planet itself is in a life-threatening situation of such magnitude that we are all imperilled? Could it be that only when the planet experiences a sufficiently acute near-death crisis on a universal scale that the collective consciousness of the planet will experience a shift to a higher level that will enable the entire human family to live in love and peace?

Whatever the answer may be, the role of transpersonal psychology in forwarding the possibilities of this transformation process in the immediate future (by recognising and accepting the need for understanding and in providing a caring environment where these embryonic developments can evolve into their fullest potential) is truly a service to humanity. NDEs of themselves are not automatically transformative; much depends on how the experience is interpreted and integrated.

We have seen how the obvious transformation that comes about in the lives of near-death survivors that have had a core experience tends to be both dramatic and profound. To the person who has experienced the subjectively undeniable view of the beauty of the cosmos and gained the understanding that one is an indissoluble part of that splendour, the means by which that insight is gained becomes irrelevant. It would seem that, however the NDE is brought about, the prime purpose of returning to physical life is to gain an opportunity to try to live life in accordance with the knowledge obtained while on the threshold of death. The ontological view of human existence is the understanding most NDErs seem to have of their experience and explains why their universal interpretation advances life promotion.

But we do not need nearly to die in order to experience a higher spiritual reality. The idea that the afterlife can be considered in objective terms is one of the reasons for this misconception. When one realises that heaven and hell are not places to which we 'go' when our earthly life is ended, but rather a 'state' which we create ourselves and which can be changed by us at any moment, one starts to understand that instead of 'going' to a place in space, we find ourselves instead in one of the 'planes' of existence that abide in our 'world within'. This state of activity which resides in the eternal energy of the spirit is the one which, according to Ramacharaka in his book *The Life Beyond Death*, the cosmos 'lives, moves and has its being'.

When this is realised it puts the responsibility for our future firmly in our own hands here and now and one begins to realise that no one but oneself can provide the measure of one's own life's purpose and meaning. This is the realisation that has come to many mystics down the ages and which is now being experienced by ordinary men and women via the agency of the collective consciousness of the universal mind on an ever-increasing scale. Enlightened beings all have their own ways of attempting to express the ineffable, but the realisation of this truth is expressed with beautiful simplicity by Omar Khayyam in *The Rubaiyat* when he says:

> I sent my Soul through the Invisible,
> Some letter of that After-life to spell;
> And after many days my Soul returned and said,
> Behold, Myself am Heav'n and Hell.

# APPENDIX I

Place of interview. . . . . . . . . . . . . . . . . . . . . . . . . . . . .
Date. . . . . . . . .

Referred by. . . . . . . . . . . . . . . . . . . . . . . . . . . . . . . . . . . . . . .

Name of Respon-
dent. . . . . . . . . . . . . . . . . . . . . . . . . . . . . . . . . . . . . . .

Age. . . . . . . . . .Sex. . . . . . . . . .Nationality-
. . . . . . . . . .Race. . . . . . . . . .

Marital status:
    married. . . . . . .single. . . . . .
    divorced. . . . . . .widowed. . . . . . .

Occupation. . . . . . . . . . . . . . . . . . . . . . . . . . . . . . . . . . . . .

Baptised religion. . . . . . . . . . . . . . . . . . .Current religion. . . . . . . . . . . . . .

Circumstances of NDE:
    illness. . . . . . . . . . . accident. . . . . . . . . . . suicide
attempt. . . . . . . . . . .
date. . . . . . . . . location. . . . . . . . . . . . . . . . . . . . . . . . . . . .
    specific conditions. . . . . . . . . . . . . . . . . . . . . . . . . . . . . . . . . .

Free narrative of experience (tape recorded when possible).

Questions following respondents' recollection of events to elicit any
memory of special or unusual feelings, perceptions, imagery, etc., and
reactions to them.

1  How difficult is it to put into words?

2  What perceptions of dying or death did you experience? Did you for
   instance hear yourself pronounced dead?

3  What feelings and sensations can you remember having at the time of your NDE? Do you remember any feelings of movement or hearing any unusual sounds?

4  Did you have any feelings of separation from your physical body? If so, can you describe this experience and say how you felt at the time? (Do you remember having any thoughts when you were in this state?)

5  When you were out of your body, where were you? Did you have another body? If so, can you describe it? While you were in this state, what were your perceptions of time and space? How did you perceive your weight? Were you able to do things that you would not normally be able to do in your physical body? Do you remember being aware of any tastes or odours? Were your senses of sight and sound altered in any way? Did you experience a sense of loneliness at any time, and if so in what way?

6  During your episode did you at any time encounter other individuals, living or dead? If so, who were they? What occurred? Did they communicate and, if so, what and how? Why do you think they communicated what they did? How did you feel in their presence?

7  Was any light, glow or illumination experienced at any time? If so, did this light communicate anything to you and, if so, what? What did you make of this light and how did it affect you? Did you sense any force or power of wisdom and love connected with it? Did you encounter any religious figures, guardian spirits, angelic beings, etc.? Did you encounter any frightening images or demonic beings? Did you sense any evil force?

8  At the time of the experience, did your life – or scenes from your life – appear to you as mental images or memories? If so, what did you feel and did you think you learned something from this experience? Did you at any time feel judged?

9  Did you have any sense of reaching some kind of boundary or threshold? If so, can you describe this and also what feelings or thoughts you recall having at this time? Do you have a sense of what this boundary might represent or mean?

10  When you found yourself back in your body, what were your first thoughts or feelings? Did you want to come back? Do you recall how you returned or why you didn't remain on the other side?

### Life changes

1  Do you feel this experience has changed you in any way or altered
   your attitude towards life? If so, how? Are you for instance more or
   less positive than you were before? If more, can you say if this includes
   an enhanced feeling of self-esteem? Do you feel any sense of personal
   renewal or rebirth? If so, how do you express this? Do you find your
   attitude towards others has changed? If so, does this include
   intensified feelings of compassion and tolerance towards others? Do
   you feel a need to be of service to others and does this include a sense
   of mission or purpose? How important are material considerations to
   you now compared with before?

2  Before your near-death episode, how afraid of death were you? Do
   you fear death more or less than you did before, or do you feel the
   same as you did prior to your experience? Has the experience changed
   your attitude towards suicide? What is your understanding of death
   and what does it mean to you?

3  What is your belief in life after death? Has your conviction been
   altered in any way by your experience and, if so, how? What were
   your views concerning heaven and hell before your near-death
   episode and how has your experience affected these views, if at all?

4  How important would you say religion is to you? Do you feel the
   experience has altered your religious attitude and, if so, how? What is
   your belief in God? Would you say your belief has changed and, if so,
   how? What was your concept of God before and is it the same now?

5  Did you have any knowledge about NDEs prior to your own? To
   what extent, if at all, have you read about or discussed with others
   near-death or mystical experience either before or since your own
   experience? Following your near-death episode have you tried to
   discover the meaning of your experience? Have you spoken to anyone
   other than me about your experience and, if so, what was their
   reaction?

*Note* This interview schedule is a modified version of the one used for the
   Connecticut Study.

# APPENDIX II

## APPLICATIONS FOR NEAR-DEATH STUDY PRACTICE

As previously stated, I am concerned that the issues raised by this work should be disseminated to interested professional and lay people, in order that the information gained by studies of NDEs can be used to help those facing death or those who have recently been bereaved to be able more easily to come to terms with the concept of death.

To this end I have recently formed the British Branch of the International Association for Near-Death Studies (IANDS-UK) and in keeping with the aims and objectives of the association conduct the following activities:

1 Death, dying and rebirth workshops, designed to facilitate the application of knowledge emerging from research of NDEs, in order to show how we can live life more abundantly.
2 Provide a counselling service for NDErs in order that they can talk freely about their experience and explore the potential for transformation and self-actualisation arising out of their near-death episode, through the interpretation and integration of what they have undergone.
3 Disseminate information at conferences and seminars for professional colleagues, in order to encourage the subject of near-death and related phenomena to reach into the more orthodox medical echelons, so that in time it may come to be incorporated into death education programmes in appropriate settings such as hospices, for the benefit of patients. (What psychological counselling is currently available is provided for the benefit of the staff, in order to enable them to resolve their own fear of death, so that they are able to function more efficiently in the routine care of the dying.)

People wishing to join the International Association for Near-Death Studies or who would like information about out current activities should write to:

> IANDS (U.K.)
> P.O. Box 193
> London SW1K 9JZ

# BIBLIOGRAPHY

These references include books read by the author for their thematic content but not directly quoted in the text.

Aurobindo, S. and the Mother, *Death and Rebirth*, Aurobindo Society, 1972.

Benton, R.G., *Death and Dying*, Van Nostrand Reinhold, 1978.

Bentov, I., *Stalking the Wild Pendulum*, E.P. Dutton & Co., 1977.

Blackmore, S., *Beyond the Body*, Granada Publishing, 1983.

Boisen, A., *The Exploration of the Inner World*, Harper & Row, 1936.

Borgia, A., *Life in the World Unseen*, Psychic Press Ltd. 1954.

Bucke, R.M., *Cosmic Consciousness*, E.P. Dutton & Co., 1969.

Burr, H.S., *Blueprint for Immortality*, Neville Spearman, 1972.

Capra, F., *The Tao of Physics*, Fontana Collins, 1976.

Cerminara, G., *Many Mansions*, Neville Spearman, 1967.

Cerminara, G., *The World Within*, C.W. Daniel, 1973.

Coxhead, N., *Mindpower*, Heinemann, 1964.

Dean, S.R., 'The Confluence of Psychiatry and Mysticism', *World Institute Council*, 1974.

Drury, N., *The Shaman and the Magician*, Routledge & Kegan Paul, 1982.

Fenwick, P., 'The brain and the mystery of mystical experience', *Chimo*, vol. 7, no. 8, 1981.

Ferguson, M., 'A new perspective on reality', *Brain/Mind Bulletin*, 1978.

Ferguson, M., *The Aquarian Conspiracy*, Routledge & Kegan Paul, 1981.

Frazer, J.G., *The Illustrated Golden Bough*, London, Macmillan, 1978.

Freemantle, R. and Trungpa, C., *The Tibetan Book of the Dead*, Shambhala, 1975.

Fromm, E., *The Fear of Freedom*, Routledge & Kegan Paul, 1960.

Gallup, G. Jnr, *Adventures in Immortality*, Souvenir Press, 1983.

Gibran, K., *The Prophet*, Heinemann, 1926.

Gennep A. van., *The Rights of Passage*, Routledge & Kegan Paul, 1960.

Green, C., 'Out-of-the-body experiences', Institute of Psychophysical Research, 1968.

Grof, S., *Realms of the Human Unconscious*, E.P. Dutton & Co., 1976.

Grof, S. and Grof C., *Beyond Death*, Thames & Hudson, 1980.

Grof, S. and Halifax, J., *The Human Encounter with Death*, Dutton, 1977.

Haich, E., *Initiation*, George Allen & Unwin, 1965.

Haich, E., *Sexual Energy and Yoga,* George Allen & Unwin, 1972.

Haraldsson, E. and Osis, K., *At the Hour of Death,* Avon, New York, 1977.

Hay, D., *Exploring Inner Space,* Penguin Books, 1982.

Head, J. and Cranston, S.L., *The Phoenix Fire Mystery,* Crown Publishers Inc., 1977.

Huxley, A., *The Perennial Philosophy,* Chatto & Windus, 1946.

Jung, C., *Synchronicity: An Acausal Connecting Principle, Collected Works,* 8, 47, Bollingen Series XX, Princeton, 1960.

Jung, C., *Man and His Symbols,* Aldus Books, 1964.

Jung, C. *Memories, Dreams, Reflections,* Collins and Fount Paperbacks, 1977.

Koestler, A., *The Roots of Coincidence,* Vintage Books, 1972.

Krishna, G. *Kundalini,* Shambhala, 1971.

Krishna, G., *Higher Consciousness,* Taraporevala Sons & Co., 1974.

Kubler-Ross, E., *On Death and Dying,* Tavistock Publications, 1970.

Kubler-Ross, E., *Death: the Final Stages of Growth,* Prentice Hall Inc., 1978.

Kubler-Ross, E., *To Live Until We Say Goodbye,* Prentice Hall Inc., 1978.

Kuhn, T.S., *The Structure of Scientific Revolutions,* University of Chicago Press, 1962.

Lilly, J.C., *The Centre of the Cyclone,* Julian Press, 1972.

Lindley, J.H., Bryan, S. and Conley, B., 'The evergreen study', *Anabiosis: The Journal for Near-Death Studies,* vol. 1., no. 2, 1981.

Long, M.F. *The Secret Science Behind Miracles,* Huna Research Publications, 1954.

Lum, L.C., 'Hyperventilation and anxiety states', *Journal of the Royal Society of Medicine,* vol. 74, 1981.

Maslow, A., *Towards a Psychology of Being,* D. Van Nostrand Co., 1968.

Maslow, A., *The Further Reaches of Human Nature,* Penguin Books, 1971.

Milner, D., *Explorations of Consciousness,* Neville Spearman, 1978.

Mitchell, E., *Psychic Explorations,* Putnam's, 1974.

Monroe, R.A., *Journey Out of the Body* Souvenir Press, 1972.

Moody, R.A. Jnr, *Life After Life,* Bantam Books, 1975.

Moody, R.A. Jnr, *Reflections on Life After Life,* Bantam Books, 1978.

Nixon, P.G.F., 'The human function curve; with special reference to cardiovascular disorders', *Counselling News,* 23, 8, 1978.

Noyes, R. Jnr. and Kletti, R., 'The experience of dying from falls', *Omega,* 3, 1972.

Noyes, R. Jnr and Kletti, R., 'Depersonalisation in the face of life-threatening danger: a description', *Psychiatry,* 39, 1976.

Perry, J., *The Far Side of Madness*, Prentice Hall, 1971.

Pribram, K.H., *Language of the Brain: Experimental Paradoxes and Principles in Neuropsychology*, Prentice Hall, 1971.

Ramacharaka, Y., *The Life Beyond Death*, Yogi Publication Society, 1937.

Rawlings, M., *Beyond Death's Door*, Nelson, 1978.

Ring, K., *Life at Death: A Scientific Investigation of the Near-Death Experience*, Coward McCann and Geohegan, 1980.

Ring, K., 'Do Suicide Survivors Report Near-Death Experiences?', Paper presented at the American Psychiatric Association, New Orleans, 1981.

Ring, K., 'Precognitive and prophetic visions in near-death experiences', *Anabiosis: The Journal for Near-Death Studies*, vol. 2, no.11, 1982.

Ring, K., *Heading Towards Omega: In Search of the Meaning of the Near-Death Experience*, William Morrow & Co., Inc., 1984.

Russell, P., *The Awakening Earth*, Routledge & Kegan Paul, 1982.

Sabom, M., *The Near-Death Experience: A Medical Perspective*, Lippincott, 1982.

Sabom, M. and Kreutiger, S., 'Physicians evaluate the near-death experience', *The Journal of the Florida Medical Association*, 1977.

Sabom, M., *Recollections of Death*, Corgi Books, 1982.

Sannella, L., *Kundalini – Psychosis or Transcendence?*, Dakin, 1976.

Sheldrake, R., *A New Science of Life*, Granada, 1983.

Simonton, O.C. and Simonton, S., *Getting Well Again*, Bantam Books, 1980.

Stearn, J., *The Sleeping Prophet*, Frederick Muller, 1968.

Steiner, R., *Links Between the Living and the Dead*, Anthroposophical Publishing Co., 1973.

Tart, C., *Out-of-the-Body Experiences: Psychic Exploration*, Putnam's, 1974.

Tart, C., *Transpersonal Psychologies*, Routledge & Kegan Paul, 1978.

Vasiliev, L.L.*Experiments in Distant Influence*, Wildwood House, 1963.

Wheeler, D., *Journey to the Other Side*, Temp Books, 1976.

Wilber, K., *The Atman Project*, Theosophical Publishing House, 1980.

Wilber, K., *Up from Eden*, Routledge & Kegan Paul, 1983.

Wilson, F.A., *Alchemy as a Way of Life*, C.W. Daniel Co., 1973.

Woldben, A., *After Nostradamus*, Neville Spearman, 1973.

Yogananda, P., *Autobiography of a Yogi*, Rider and Co., 1969.

Yukteswar, S., *The Holy Science*, Self-Realisation Fellowship, 1977.

Zukav, G., *The Dancing Wu Li Masters*, Morrow, 1979.

# Index